BETTER ANSWERS

BETTER ANSWERS

Written Performance That Looks Good and Sounds Smart

Ardith Davis Cole

Stenhouse Publishers
Portland, Maine

Stenhouse Publishers
www.stenhouse.com

Library of Congress Cataloging-in-Publication Data
Cole, Ardith Davis.
  Better answers : written performance that looks good and sounds
smart / Ardith Davis Cole. -- 2nd ed.
      p. cm.
  Includes bibliographical references.
  ISBN 978-1-57110-748-0 (alk. paper)
  1. Language arts (Elementary)--United States. 2. Language arts (Middle
school)--United States. 3. Test-taking skills--Study and teaching
(Elementary)--United States. 4. Test-taking skills--Study and teaching
(Middle school)--United States. I. Title.
  LB1576.C5766 2009
  372.60973--dc22
                              2008035117

Cover design, interior design, and typesetting by Designboy Creative Group

Manufactured in the United States of America on acid-free, recycled paper
15 14 13 12 11 10 09   10 9 8 7 6 5 4 3 2

This book is dedicated to my children, Brad, Jen, and Heather,
and my grandchildren, Cameron, Delanie,
Makenzie, and Ashleigh—
all of whom continue to give me lots of practice in constructing
"better answers" to their ongoing questions.

CONTENTS

CD CONTENTS

FOLDER: Charts and Visuals

FOLDER: Resources

PREFACE TO THE SECOND EDITION

It was the first year of our state's new assessments, but we weren't worried. Our kids had been taking reading, math, and writing tests for many years. So when we heard that the students would be writing on the reading tests, we responded, "No problem! They know how to write."

Were we in for a surprise!

Sound familiar?

It may not have sounded familiar seven years ago when the first edition of this book was published. But now, the majority of teachers in the United States have experienced this same shock—the one that occurs when students take their first high-stakes tests on which they must construct *written* responses.

SLIGHTLY OVERWHELMED

In some cases, these assessment changes have happened so quickly that they've left us teachers breathless, filled with anxieties. Reading a brief passage on a multiple-choice test and then selecting one of four given answers is very different from what students must do on the tests of the twenty-first century. Students of the past who could read did not have to be able to write to score well on district and state tests. They merely had to color in bubbles or circle letters or phrases. But when a child's reading or science knowledge is assessed through his or her writing, it adds a whole new dimension to testing. In the past ten years, we've moved students from recall to restate to respond and reflect—a mighty task for all concerned.

LITERACY SPECIALIST, FIX THEM!

Just how mighty this task was became clear when my school was notified of the students who had not met the standards on the grade 4 state literacy assessment.

As the school's literacy coach, I was asked to bring those eighteen students up to proficiency level. As soon as the tests were returned to us, I investigated the performance of each of the students with a fine-tooth comb. It wasn't long before commonalities in their responses emerged. I didn't know it then, but locating those common errors was a turning point on our path to success.

THE PROCESS UNFOLDS

The first thing I noticed about the students' responses was that many of them did not seem to even know what the question was. They appeared to have answered a different question! Thus, Step 1 of the Better Answer protocol began to take shape: Ask them to simply restate the question or petition.

Next I noticed how shallow the students' responses were. Some wrote little more than one sentence. I'd often heard teachers suggest, "Write more," but it never worked. This problem took a while to solve, but finally, it hit me. An answer must *first* be only a general—a gist—response, which would then usher in the evidential details to support it. Of course! *The restatement and gist become the main idea that introduces the response.*

Once we had the restatement and gist down pat, the rest was a downhill slide. That's because all those evidential details evolve directly out of the main idea. After that, all we had to do was add a conclusion. Three easy steps: introduction, details, conclusion.

HOORAY! POSITIVE RESULTS!

The students, their classroom teachers, and I implemented the protocol over the following four months, and on the next state test, ten of the eighteen intervention students met the grade 5 standards. Those results, as well as the students' positive responses to the protocol, prompted me to share the strategies with others—others who also had success using it.

Denise Vassar, a fourth-grade teacher from City of Buffalo Schools, wrote to me, "This is the first year I had students score a 4 [the highest score]! My students scored 2s, 3s, and 4s (no 1s), an overall improvement from last year. The struggling readers who were in the 1 zone scored a 2 and I know that's because of [the Better Answer formula and your note-taking tips]. . . . When you make learning fun and interesting and show confidence in their ability to learn, the students will make every effort to do their best."

Since publishing that first edition of *Better Answers*, I have continued to work with teachers and kids across the country. I'm always grateful when teachers share positive results, and some of their celebrations have even been published. A district newspaper from Wells, New York, interviewed teachers who were using *Better Answers*. "'This approach is so structured, so easy,' Mrs. Wilcox explained. 'The program really works. Student writing skills are improving tremendously with the sandwich method'" (Montgomery County BOCES 2005, 1).

APPLICABILITY ACROSS GRADE LEVELS AND SUBJECTS

Because of its reliable structure, the Better Answer protocol has been successfully implemented from grade 2 through grade 12. What's more, many schools across the country, including those in rural communities and inner cities, have used it throughout middle school and high school subjects. We've discovered that a sound response can possess similar attributes whether it's related to a science prompt or one from social studies or reading. This protocol, therefore, offers a common structure with similar strategies and tools that support cross-grade and cross-subject dialogues.

WHAT'S NEW IN THE SECOND EDITION?

You may be wondering, if the first edition of *Better Answers* worked so well, why change it? Let me explain.

The more I used the process and talked with teachers and students, the more new ideas began to take shape and old ideas morphed. Eventually, I decided to make the following changes:

- reorganize the book so it's easier to use
- add a very important chapter related to prompts
- add a whole chapter full of ideas for what to do when you're baffled
- include a CD with everything a busy teacher needs to make his or her job easier

I hope you'll find that using the second edition is like visiting with an old friend whom you've not seen for a number of years. You sense a friendly familiarity, yet there are many exciting changes you'd like to explore.

THE GOOD REMAINS

First of all, know that I've kept all of the first edition's goodies:

- the Activities sections
- the Assessment and Conferring sections
- the story-like vignettes
- all those great charts (with some revisions and some new charts added)
- the handy classroom samples and examples
- the print and Web resources
- the appendix material

As a matter of fact, I not only kept the good ideas and tools, I've also packaged some of them in a more convenient manner on the CD that is included with the second edition—but read on, because I describe this nice addition in a later paragraph.

THE REORGANIZATION OF THE BETTER ANSWER PROTOCOL

The reliable, step-by-step process of the Better Answer protocol remains in the second edition, but I've reorganized it. The first edition described five separate steps in the Better Answer protocol:

1. Restate the question.
2. Construct a gist answer.
3. Use details to support your answer.
4. Stay on the topic.
5. Use proper conventions.

Although the new book addresses each of these steps, they are integrated into the book's three major parts:

- Part I Prewriting: Setting the Stage for Success
- Part II Writing: Constructing a Response
- Part III Postwriting: Assessment and Our Response to It

Let's take a quick peek inside each part to see what's new and what's not.

Prewriting: Setting the Stage for Success

At the top of my revision list sits a focus on understanding the prompt, which is absolutely crucial to constructing a comprehensive and correct response. The first edition *did* mention aspects of the prompt; however, it did *not* go into detail regarding this essential piece of the process. That's why the prewriting section offers you a crash course in analyzing prompts. Students who cannot competently analyze the prompt often start their response journey headed in the wrong direction.

First of all, it's imperative that students understand the difference between *text-based prompts* and *self-based prompts*. Furthermore, they'll need to mindfully determine and use the prompt's components, which may include *background information*, *petitions*, and/or *questions*. Each of these has relevant subcomponents—any of which can make or break a response. It is only when students understand how to deal with a prompt's components that they will be able to direct their pens toward an appropriate response.

Writing: Constructing a Response

Part II more closely mirrors the first edition's Better Answer Sandwich. The sandwich itself remains intact, and this edition gives it the status it merits. The Better Answer protocol had five steps in the first edition. This revised protocol adheres to the Better Answer Sandwich's three steps:

Step 1: Develop an Introduction
Step 2: Build a Body of Details
Step 3: Draw a Conclusion

One chapter is devoted to each step, with some new ideas and activities included to enrich the whole. Each chapter is comprehensively presented in a way that helps the steps unfold one out of the other, making the process easy to teach and easy to learn.

Lessons Are Offered for Both Self-Based and Text-Based Responses

Another change you'll notice throughout the second edition is the manner in which lessons are focused on either *self-based* or *text-based* responses. The prompt chapter describes the differences between these two, and then lessons focus on one or the other—but rarely both at the same time. Some states label these two kinds of writing *narrative* and *expository*, but some also entangle the two. This edition untangles some of those knots by presenting the threads that hold self-based and text-based writing intact.

Postwriting: Assessment and Our Response to It

After students draft their answer, it is time to move on to the postwriting process: assessing the writing and then, most importantly, *responding* to the assessment of the writing. For the students, postwriting means rereading to assess in order to edit or revise. For the teacher, the postwriting phase means using assessment to respond to students' individual needs.

Yet, both students and teachers should be able to rely on a common assessment tool. So, as with the first edition, I offer the Better Answer Rubric, which will point students and teachers toward the writer's greatest need. Other tools, such as teacher monitoring sheets, help professionals keep track of individual and class strengths and weaknesses.

It is important to emphasize that the Better Answer Rubric, or any assessment tool for that matter, should not be an end point in the writing process. Instead, student growth occurs when we use the findings of the assessment tool to refocus our teaching to meet students' needs and build their skills. This is why Part III is titled "Assessment and Our Response to It."

Conventions

Strategies and ideas related to conventions can now be found in Part III, Chapters 8 and 9. Conventions are no longer a separate step in the process. Why, you might ask? We both know that conventions are undoubtedly important. They help writers look good and allow their work to more easily be read. However, conventions are related to editing. They are something writers focus on *after* they've got it all down. How can we assess our spelling or grammar unless it's already been written?

A considerable number of writing assessments now score conventions as a separate entity, and most subject-area tests indicate that conventions should *not* even be scored or counted. Nevertheless, a responder's spelling, grammar, handwriting, spacing, punctuation, and such will influence most people who read his or her response. So even though conventions aren't supposed to count, they always do. That's why they're included in the Better Answer Rubric and addressed in the postwriting part of this book.

A Handy, New Response Resource to Help Answer Your Questions

One of the best things about Part III is offered in the book's last (voluminous) chapter. This section grew out of the first edition's Chapter 4, "Stay on the Topic," but I've put that chapter to a better use. You see, it was so full of good ideas for helping students who go astray that it provoked a reinvention of its former self. It's been woven into an entire section of suggestions for those times when teachers are at a loss for what to do. I've dubbed Part III, Chapter 9, "What to Do When . . . : Responding to Assessment." A brief sampling is found below.

What to do when . . .

- writers lack a sense of audience
- writers have trouble with the conventions of language
- writers compose a shallow response

You'll find dozens of ideas to make your job of responding a bit easier. That's why you'll want to keep it handy for quick reference.

It's in this final chapter that I offer you all my tricks of the trade—a trade that's so rewarding it keeps me hooked, even after all these years.

AND ONE FINAL VERY SPECIAL NEW ITEM: THE CD

When I do workshops and presentations, I know how handy it is to have everything right there on my computer—there for the sharing. It was after one of my Ohio workshops that I realized, "The *teachers* should have all these bells and whistles on *their* computers too!"

So this new edition comes with a CD that will support your teaching and the students' learning—everything (and more) that you'll need to teach the Better Answers protocol, its steps, and its strategies. Just click and you'll have

- lesson plans for every lesson;
- classroom PowerPoint lesson slides;
- charts and other visuals;
- sample text-based and self-based texts, prompts, and student responses;
- assessment and monitoring tools;
- print resource bibliographies;
- live-link resources (including links to state websites' prompts and students' responses, plus sites with living prompts).

From lesson plans to live links to a variety of visuals, it's all there to help lighten your load.

There are several ways you can find material on the CD. First, the CD Contents at the front of the book lists all documents and files on the CD, organized by the folder that contains them.

Second, as you read the book, you'll see cross-references to the contents of the CD in the margins. These CD icons look like the one at the right. They'll point you to the section of the CD where you'll find the slides, charts, or lessons relevant to the topic being discussed in the book. The book's appendix contains much of the material that's on the CD, so you'll have a quick and easy visual reference as you read. The appendixes are also organized just like the content of the CD, so you can find what you need easily.

Third, in addition to being referred to the CD as you read the book, you can peruse the contents of the CD separately, ideally after you've read the book and understand the way the Better Answer protocol works. Orientation screens and a "How to Use the CD" document on the CD itself will help you navigate to find the lesson plan, chart, or PowerPoint presentation you need.

AN INVITATION

A few years ago, School 9 in Rochester, New York, invited me in to share the success they'd had using *Better Answers*. One of the things I'll always remember about that day was my experience with a third grader who was leading me to the next classroom. As we hurried along, he turned and announced, "Ya know, I really liked your book."

"You read it?" I asked, trying not to sound surprised.

When he responded affirmatively, I asked him what he liked about it. That nine-year-old stood there in the hallway and cogently described the attributes of *Better Answers*. Truly, a moving and memorable experience.

I share this little story because I believe it demonstrates the simplicity of this process, this book. May it lead you and your students toward better answers. And may it offer the confidence needed to throw those test-prep workbooks into the recycling bin and instead use *Better Answers* techniques with living prompts, not only in language arts, but also in reading, science, and social studies—indeed, in all school subjects.

ACKNOWLEDGMENTS

First and foremost, I wish to thank the students in whose classrooms I constructed and implemented various phases of the Better Answer protocol: the group of fifth graders from Maplemere Elementary School in Amherst, New York, who walked with me as I stumbled and bumbled my way through the first leg of this journey; the kids in grades 3, 4, and 8 at Buffalo's International School 45 who helped me shade and hue the protocol to accommodate a multitude of individual differences; the kids in Barb McKay's fourth grade, who, amongst other things, even lent a hand in creating the book's assessment samples; and all those other students in the Buffalo and Sweet Home schools, each of whom added a small piece to this whole. A very special thanks goes to the fourth graders from Buffalo Schools 45 and 4, for it is their beautiful faces that grace this book. And finally, the new chapter on prompts took shape primarily through my experiences with students at Mountain View Elementary School in Port Townsend, Washington. Thanks to all of you!

Heartfelt thanks also go to several New York colleagues: Maplemere fourth-grade teacher Barb McKay, whose open door and mindful questions continue to draw me in; the principal of School 45 in Buffalo, Colleen Caroda, who so graciously invited me into their community; the curriculum director at School 45, Mary Ann Hopfer, my Better Answer cheerleader, who pours into my cup until my confidence runs right over the edge; the fourth-grade teachers at School 45 and School 4 in Buffalo, Denise Vassar, Gwen Humphrey, Darlene McFadden, Maria Fasolino, and Mary Weiss, who are now "the pros"; and Lockport Middle School English teacher Renee Knight, who so graciously responded to my first draft (which was a lot longer!).

And now, for this second edition, I'd like to also thank my Port Townsend, Washington, colleagues Mary Manning, Diane Frame, and Mary Wilson, all of whom have lent a hand and a listening ear. Since the publication of the first edition of *Better Answers*, I've met many wonderful educators across the country, teachers who have shared their related experiences and ideas. Surely they too have helped sculpt this new edition. What wonderful colleagues!

And of course, a big celebration hug goes to my family and friends: to Elaine Garan, who is always there and never minds hearing drafts read over the phone; and to my own children and their families, who give me the inspiration, confidence, and love that all writers need. A special thank-you hug goes to my talented daughter Heather, who gifted me with the CD's artwork. Two great big hugs go to my grandchildren Delanie and Cameron, and son Brad, all of whom patiently cooperated with my end-of-project needs.

I'm honored that one of the world's finest environmental groups, the World Wildlife Fund, and editor Ste graciously offered full articles for the CD so that students can tackle some real issues. The Wilderness Society and Nature Conservancy have articles included too. I hope students are drawn to service in these wonderful nonprofit organizations.

I also want to offer a "hindsight" thank-you to Anne Fullerton, who edited my first book and from whom I learned more than any writing course could ever teach. I think of Anne again and again as her knowledgeable guidance continues to guide my pen.

And last, but certainly not least, I want to extend my sincere appreciation to the helpful and patient individuals at Stenhouse Publishers: to Philippa Stratton, who immediately believed in *Better Answers* and, along with the reviewers of the early draft, gave direction and focus for that first book and then invited me into this second edition; to Tom Seavey, a longtime professional friend; and to Sean McGee and mindful, meticulous Erin Trainer, who walked me through the final stages of the two editions. I also want to take this opportunity to thank Nate Butler, Chuck Lerch, and Doug Kolmar, Stenhouse managers who have been so helpful over my years with the company. For all of these terrific people, I am grateful.

My gratitude also goes to you, the reader, who decided to try the protocol on for size. May your own journey into better answers be as exciting and rewarding an experience as mine has been.

PREWRITING:

SETTING THE STAGE
FOR SUCCESS

PART 1

CHAPTER 1

GETTING STARTED WITH THE FOUNDATIONS FOR SUCCESS

Learning to become literate ought to be as uncomplicated and barrier-free as possible.
—Brian Cambourne, *The Whole Story*

Almost everything we learn begins with baby steps. We practice golfing be-haviors at the driving range and the putting green before we attempt eighteen holes. Children use training wheels as Mom or Dad hangs on to the seat—and before they ride bicycles independently across town to a friend's house. We learn to swim in three feet of water, not the deep end of the pool. Anytime children or adults are learning a new task, it's made easier by eliminating the variables that might distract, frighten, or confuse them.

It therefore seems reasonable that students will also learn the steps in this process more easily and more confidently if we initially use two guideposts:

enticing topics for self-based writing, in which students are asked to draw from their own life experiences; and simplistic text for text-based writing, in which students draw from a given reading passage in framing their response.

Use Enticing Topics for Self-Based Writing

For self-based writing, I always start with a topic that I know will capture my audience. What's a topic kids want to investigate? One thing I know for sure is that kids always want to know about us, their teachers—what we do in our spare time, who we live with, where we live, and so much more. So a tiny look inside the life of their teacher is the topic for my initial prompt and its response.

Once we really get into self-based writing, I tend to search for topics in the real world of students, rather than school's test world—living, not lifeless, prompts. The more interesting the topic, the better they'll learn and write.

Use Simplistic Texts for Text-Based Writing

Why have students wrestle with textual content when they are learning a new process? Why complicate matters? There is no reason to do so, of course.

That assumption proved correct—even for teachers learning the process during staff development workshops. That's why old, well-known tales, such as "Little Red Riding Hood," are the grist for text-based modeling sessions and for the students' first attempts at using text-based writing strategies. These familiar tales create the perfect background for success in learning response techniques. Novices do not have to wade through tough text while learning a new strategy, yet the entire class works together from a common source. This way, *they can concentrate on the process itself*. Old tales become our driving range and putting green, common anchors to be referenced again and again.

Although most children are familiar with tales such as "Little Red Riding Hood" and "The Three Little Pigs," it is still important to read a version of each story before using it (see the CD and the appendix). We can never assume that everyone in the group knows these stories, even though they are found in many cultures across the world. Furthermore, because the Better Answer protocol works effectively with both nonfiction and fiction, using these fictional tales does not deter the transfer to more difficult, nonfiction text later. The same steps—the same process—are used for any brief, extended, essay, or constructed response. The basic protocol provides a beginning structure for both text-based and self-based writing. As a matter of fact, the process works just as well in the real world, on the job, or wherever written response occurs.

Monitoring Spreadsheets

A BASELINE ASSESSMENT

I usually suggest that teachers use one of the text and prompt samples included on the CD and in the appendix, to obtain a formative baseline assessment *before* beginning the process of teaching the Better Answer Protocol. The longer samples, the fairy tales, work well for grades 5 through 8, and the shorter ones, the fables, for grades 3 and 4 (even grade 2). I ask teachers to simply read one of the tales aloud to their students and then have students respond to one of my question or petition prompts. We then tuck these preassessments away. After we finish teaching the entire protocol, we do a postassessment in the same manner. Then, we evaluate both their pre- and postassessments using the Better Answer Rubric. It will be a time to pat everyone on the back—teacher included!

Eventually, you can log those first results on a class spreadsheet to monitor the group's progress (see the CD and the appendix). To ground your formative assessment results, individual monitoring spreadsheets not only provide a record of the present way station at which each student resides, but also will show quite clearly the progress he or she has made since the beginning of the *Better Answers* journey. Yet, the best part of this experience is sharing the results with the kids. What a confidence builder the Better Answer protocol is! And we teachers know that confidence grows competence. So don't forget to give that preassessment.

MODELING IS MANDATORY

You'll quickly notice that lessons are introduced through modeling, think-alouds, and shared writing experiences. Stephanie Harvey (1998) calls these initial, supported, memorable experiences "anchoring," because each can remain a common reference experience for the whole class. So when teachers keep charts on which they've modeled writing, such anchors become a handy support for later reference. I rely heavily upon those anchor charts throughout the year. It's quite usual to hear a teacher say something like, "Remember when we developed an answer to that 'Three Little Pigs' question? How did we do the details then? Check our anchor chart on the wall."

Furthermore, students need to observe how we teachers think when composing so that they can emulate our writing behaviors. For students to reenact our moves and thoughts, they need to understand how we mindfully wind our way, step by step, through a process. Learning is scaffolded up an avenue of success when we take the onus off the learners, allowing them to just listen and learn without the threat of "doing it wrong" hanging over them.

I especially like to demonstrate that the act of writing is not a neat and tidy process; instead, things sometimes get pretty jumbled. Learners need to see us drop back and press our restart buttons, and demonstration is the best way to show this. I believe modeling is the most important aspect of this entire instructional process—the one thing that should never be omitted, the teaching strategy that makes a huge difference. When students are not doing well, I know it's usually because I didn't model enough.

A Gradual Release of Process Ownership

No matter what the grade level is, I try to teach each step using the following *gradual release* sequence (Pearson and Gallagher 1983). At first, I'm in total control as I demonstrate the process for students. However, I gradually pass that ownership along to the learners until they are in control of the process. A website by John Holly (http://home.earthlink.net/~jhholly/gradualrelease.htm) offers an at-a-glance visual of the gradual release model, but I've also described it below.

A Gradual Release Instructional Framework
- Teacher models Strategy A (for example, Step 1 in the Better Answer protocol) while students watch and listen.
- Teacher gradually invites students into other Strategy A examples through partnering (dyads).
- Teacher invites students into small-group settings where they can discuss new Strategy A examples.
- Students work independently on Strategy A as teacher monitors.
- Teacher continues to scaffold students gradually toward more skilled Strategy A performance through assessment and response to that assessment.

A Developmental Model Scaffolds Students into Success

The Better Answer protocol is a developmental model; that is, each step builds on the previous one until the process is complete. Consequently, it's a good fit with the gradual release instructional model. Both rely heavily upon what came before.

In a developmental model, the first step is so easy that even struggling students establish a level of confidence. Steps sequentially become more difficult, but each evolves out of the previous one, producing a kind of scaffolding effect. This, along with all of the concrete organizers and other supports, helps students slide from the prompt to the three-step protocol and right on to success.

Certainly, constructing a written response is not the only skill in life that is better learned through this kind of scaffolded instruction. It's a basic confidence builder, and without confidence it is tough to look good and sound smart.

LOOKIN' GOOD! SOUNDIN' SMART!

One of the essential things that I want kids to know is that, when the stakes are high, their entire performance is about lookin' good and soundin' smart. There are definitely times throughout life when we need to look good and sound smart. Taking tests in school is only one of those times.

We also need to look good and sound smart at job interviews, on college and employment applications, when speaking with a high official, when being interviewed before the public, or when attempting to explain why we want our money back on broken merchandise. Indeed, there are many times in life when it's important to use formal language and to present ourselves in a somewhat different manner than we do at home with our family and friends. At such times, we change the register of our language. And so it should be.

The Better Answer protocol will help students do this. It will help them look good and sound smart.

GETTING STARTED

Each chapter in this book begins by describing how to model a particular aspect of the Better Answer process for students. Examples and samples of prompts, texts, writing, and student responses can be transferred right out of the book or off the CD and into the classroom—examples I have used a gazillion times and am still using. Readers will also find classroom vignettes that provide lively examples of how each step plays out during a lesson. These "written movies" will help you internalize the process.

The complementary activities interspersed throughout the book offer review, reinforcement, or extension of the presented strategies. For some steps in the process, reinforcement through the activities is necessary, because students need more practice. But when responders appear to have conquered a particular step fairly easily, the review or extension activities serve as a different kind of resource. Some activities connect to content-area learning and help students transfer parts of the protocol to specific subjects. They extend the process. This variety of options offers handy resources for all teachers.

KEEP THE CD HANDY AND USE THE APPENDIXES FOR QUICK REFERENCE

The CD offers everything you'll need to teach the Better Answer protocol— lesson plans, PowerPoint slides, charts, resources, prompts, articles, stories . . . everything. So before you jump into Chapter 2, "Understanding the Prompt," surf through the CD's menu screens and click on a few items of interest. That preview will provide a useful overview as you're reading each chapter. Furthermore, as you begin teaching the process, you'll be able to predict what's already done for you and available on the CD. Obviously, you'll make changes to suit your own needs and students. Nevertheless, the CD can save you tons of time, because everything is but a click away.

We've designed the appendixes at the back of the book to match the organization of files on the CD. This way, you'll be able to flip back to the appendixes for a quick reference and then download or print the documents you need from the CD when you're ready to use them. Rather than including all of the lesson plans, PowerPoint slides, and student response samples, the appendixes provide a brief sampling. However, you can easily view, download, and print all of them from the CD.

DUMP THE TEST-PREP WORKBOOKS!

One thing is sure. There will be a whole lot more time in the day once the Better Answer protocol replaces those test-prep workbooks. After the structure is understood, this protocol will integrate right into any curriculum—science, social studies, math, technology, or reading.

In contrast, test-prep workbooks are a curriculum in and of themselves. They usurp a considerable amount of time, and yet they are not easy to integrate. For one thing, they are boring! You and I both know kids hate workbook pages.

Additionally, their narratives and text pieces are not related to your curriculum; they are related to what the test manufacturer has in mind—entities unto themselves; they apply only to tests. On the other hand, the Better Answer protocol is applicable across the curriculum—anywhere that questions are asked and answers are developed, even outside of school.

Real-World Connections

I know you'll agree that our ultimate teaching intentions should not be limited to right answers on tests. Rather, it's important to connect such learning to the privileges and rights of committed citizens in a democratic society. Essentially, that is what response writing is all about. It's about making one's voice heard, evoking change, and forging pathways to a better world. Therefore, watch for places where such connections can be made—not only my suggested connections and live links found on the CD, but also any real-world seeds that can be planted. Through these meaningful applications students develop the greatest intention to learn.

Web Resources

That's one of the major reasons I included the live links section on the CD. The links will connect you with living prompts and ways kids will *want* to write for real reasons—rather than just because the teacher says so. Plus, they are rooted in soil that's fertile for growing science, social studies, technology, the arts, and tons of other interesting subjects. So once the steps have been introduced, get real!

HOW LONG WILL THIS TAKE?

Many teachers ask about the length of time needed to implement this process. Obviously, it will vary according to age, ability, and background level of the students involved. I have taught both parts of Step 1, restating the question and composing a gist answer, in a single lesson in a third grade, and the kids exited looking like pros. But, it has also taken a week for some students to internalize that first two-part step. Integration across the curriculum definitely makes a difference. Like most skills, the more students experience the protocol, the more rapid the internalization. However, it is helpful to give continual attention to the Assessing/Conferring sections throughout the process. Then, once a step in the protocol is taught, continue by implementing the Better Answers Rubric along with response-to-writing suggestions for each student. It is through such ongoing assessments that you'll be able to predict the answer to "How long will this take?"

IT WORKS! IT WORKS!

The success of the Better Answer protocol can be seen on the faces of all those struggling responders who now use "the sandwich." Smiles reflect the pride that results from being able to independently construct a sound and acceptable written response. In the end, seeing that pride and that new level of confidence is the greatest payoff.

I've used this protocol with learners of varying ability in grades 3 through 8, including inner-city students identified as special education and ESL. When implemented step by step with lots of modeling, it works to raise levels of literacy performance on brief, extended, or essay responses with students across *all* grade levels. It even works for adults.

In an article from Rochester, New York's, *Democrat and Chronicle* (Flanigan 2005) the principal of School 20, D'Onnarae Johnson, whose school made more progress on standardized English exams than any other school in the state, contends the following:

No matter what reform model you choose, if everybody is not on board with it, then it won't be successful. Our staff was able to be led in the right direction.

That leadership, in part, has come indirectly from someone not even employed by the City School District. Literacy specialist Ardith Davis Cole, in her book *Better Answers: Written Performance That Looks Good and Sounds Smart,* outlines a step-by-step protocol for helping students meet state standards on English Language Arts exams.

THE GROUND FLOOR

The Better Answer protocol is the beginning of a never-ending journey to becoming a better response writer. It is a foundation, a ground floor. Its fundamental strategies and simplicity build the confidence to move into more complex, yet similar, tasks—tasks that will be required both in school and throughout life.

So let's begin at the beginning. And there's no better place to start than with the prompt.

CHAPTER 2

UNDERSTANDING
THE PROMPT

The answer is in the question.

—Rumi

Are the students in your school expected to read test prompts and then construct appropriate written responses? If so, the contents of this chapter can set you and your students on a path that leads to better answers—a path that begins with the prompt. For it is the prompt—written or spoken, serious or mundane, living or lifeless—that leads students directly into a better answer.

WHAT, EXACTLY, IS A PROMPT?

Regardless of venue, a prompt is *any written, graphic, or spoken message that encourages the receiver to act.* Whether or not that receiver chooses to act is another matter.

11

Most important: *Prompts are not only on tests.* We meet myriad prompts both in school and out. But no matter where they are found, their relationship with their response is close and crucial.

The Response-to-Prompt Relationship

Understanding what the prompt is asking is key to a good response. The two sides of the same coin, prompt and response, are inherently related. This is the most basic understanding students need to possess to construct a sound response, and the following activity offers an easy initial lesson.

ACTIVITY

Turning Responses into Questions

To help students understand the important relationship between questions and answers, prompts and responses, I construct a chart containing several simple responses minus the questions that evoked them. (At this early point in the process, I stick to one-sentence questions for prompts.)

1. I go to bed every night around 10 p.m.
2. My favorite food is vanilla ice cream.
3. My house is on Third Street.
4. To get to my house, you'll have to cross Broad Street, walk two blocks, and then turn left on Cedar.
5. I'm happy because I got a gift in the mail.

Read the first statement to the group, and then show how easy it is to figure out what question could have provoked that response. For example, I'd say, "Someone must have asked, 'What time do you go to bed every night?'" Invite the group into the process, and eventually, ask partners to move through the rest of the statements, turning each one inside out, converting it to the question that prompted it. Later, try turning this process around by inviting the kids to think of answers/responses that need questions. (See the Question Connections chart on the CD and in the appendix.)

Other Charts and Visuals

Prompts of All Sorts and Sizes

States label the answers to prompts in a variety of ways; they call them *brief, extended, open, essay,* or *constructed responses.* Because of the grand array of possibilities, it's necessary to carefully consider how each type of answer is defined in its particular situation.

Prompts come in many shapes and sizes too. But the space that directly follows the prompt is just as important as the prompt itself. That is, after some prompts you'll find one line, one space, indicating that a very, very brief response (or open response) is expected. Others offer a few lines, several spaces, and still others offer a whole page, or even two or three. We will never know how to construct a response without actually viewing *the space after the prompt*. In other words, one cannot judge a response without the prompt's content, nor without its physical context.

LIVING PROMPTS: THE POWER OF REAL-LIFE EXPERIENCES

Prompts that inspire student interest—ones they can personally relate to—are great teaching aids. For example, referring to a recent nutrition chapter, we might invite students to "Explain what was healthy about a meal you recently had." How much more inviting that prompt is compared with the following: "List five healthy foods and explain why they are healthy."

The first prompt would be more interesting to most of us, because it is a *living prompt*. Living prompts help connect school learning to the real world. After all, we don't want students thinking that prompts and their responses are related *only* to tests.

PROMPTS ARE EVERYWHERE

You've no doubt received some prompts within the past twenty-four hours. Within the past week, I bet you've even received some prompts for which you, yourself, constructed a written response. For example, did any message you've received prompt you to write

Prewriting: 1.1

    ____ directions of any kind?

    ____ a return memo?

    ____ a report?

    ____ an email?

    ____ an answer on a test or a survey?

    ____ a letter?

    ____ a text message?

If so, you no doubt received a prompt. Once we actually start looking for prompts, we quickly realize that, indeed, prompts *are* everywhere. The Internet abounds with them—starting with my own email inbox:

Please seize this one chance for a clean energy future. Make your voice heard. . . *(from NRDC)*

Select "change" and it should not be necessary to select "Don't show this warning again . . . " but if it appears 2 more times for the same event after selecting change each time—with at least one restart in between, then select it. *(from my computer consultant)*

Would you please email me the recipe for that pesto you made for the potluck? *(from a friend)*

The Peter Gorman Adventure Into the Heart of the Amazon and Highlands in Peru June 7-28 will fill up, so reserve your place soon for this exciting shamanic medicine plant journey. This trip is limited to 12 people. *(from www.greatmystery.org)*

Combine Cash and Miles to fly roundtrip from Seattle for as low as $109* and 20,000 WorldPerks miles . . . Seats are limited and blackout dates apply, so hurry and purchase your tickets today! *(from Northwest Airlines)*

These are but a few of the emailed prompts that I received in just *one day*. What's more, I bet students in your class are developing prompts and responding to them through other exciting avenues—like Internet chat rooms, YouTube, or even Webkinz. Ask your students to share some of these avenues. It can be the first step in helping your class understand the prompt-response relationship.

Prompts Are Everywhere

Steep your students in prompts. Collect them from everywhere. Invite the students into the collection process. There's no better way to begin an understanding of prompts than to search our daily environments for different kinds.

"Where do prompts come from?" I ask. "Let's collect as many as we can find; then we'll analyze some." I go on to make suggestions to the class: "See if your mom or dad ever receive any prompts; maybe they receive some at work. Listen to TV ads. Check your magazines. Are there prompts on your medicine bottles? Are their prompts in your DVD manual? How about on your computer? Oh, my gosh! I issued a bunch to you just now."

After a few days, we begin sharing but continue to search. Thoughts related to the prompts' similarities and differences will vary, and conclusions will vary; that doesn't matter. What does matter is that the class becomes thoroughly immersed in prompts of all kinds. An anchor chart sporting a ton of examples helps remind students that, indeed, prompts are everywhere.

STRATEGIES FOR ANALYZING A PROMPT

After the extensive experience sharing all kinds of prompts, students will realize that some prompts are simple one-liners. But it is the complexity of others that can make the response task confusing, especially for novices. Complex prompts can have several parts, each with a different indication, a different purpose, a separate instruction. Without a thorough understanding of the essential characteristics of a prompt, it's difficult to know where and how to even begin to respond. You will be able to develop better prompts, and your students will be able to construct better answers after learning about the following two aspects of prompts:

1. **Prompt Types**
   - text-based prompts
   - self-based prompts

2. **Components of Prompts**
   - prompt background information
   - prompt petitions
   - prompt questions

First things first! So let's begin with text-based and self-based prompts. Later in the chapter, I'll discuss background prompt information, prompt petitions, and prompt questions.

TEXT-BASED OR SELF-BASED?

Anytime we encounter a prompt, we need to first read the entire task to decide whether it's text- or self-based or both. That is, does the prompt direct us toward a text or texts for our response, or does it direct us toward our own life and experiences? Does the answer lie within someone else's writing and thinking, or does it lie within me, the responder? Prompts must first be read in their entirety for responders to chart a course that leads to an appropriate response, either text-based or self-based.

Prewriting: 1.1

The younger the student, the more experience he or she will need to discern the influential differences that exist from one prompt to another. To the young child, a prompt is a prompt is a prompt. And writing is writing is writing. Let's help responders delve into the differences.

Self-Based Prompts

Self-based prompts are most often found on writing assessments, in the humanities, and in the social sciences. They are used somewhat differently in each of these areas, yet they all prompt the writer to dig down inside his or her *personal* experiences and mind-stores for an idea, which can then be developed. Assessments in the humanities and the social sciences often call for personal opinions, stories, examples, or experiences. All of this suggests each student's response will vary in its content.

Self-based writing assessments vary in their intent. Their prompts call for responses that range from the imaginative to real-life experiences or possibilities. Nevertheless, most invite and reward creativity.

Some self-based prompts offer only a topic, which means the writer has much freedom. For example, a prompt may call the responder to "Write about a time that you took a trip." Quite a bit of freedom, right?

Other writing prompts offer a topic, but then define and narrow that topic. For instance, consider this one:

> Write about a time that you took a trip. Tell where you went and how you got there. Describe something exciting that happened and why you will always remember that trip.

The differences between these two prompts seem obvious to us adults, but students—who have not met a variety of prompts—may not see the more restrictive nature of the second prompt. Again, I suggest a wide variety of experiences examining all kinds of self-based prompts. But do compare them with others that are text-based.

Writing from "The Zone"

There's another realm of self-based writing that needs to be addressed before we delve into text-based. Some states have been known to give students prompts that require them to dredge the depths of imagination. Some say "writers have a *zone*, just like athletes and musicians. Space and time disappear there" (http://phantomprof.blogspot.com/2005/09/writing-workshop-lesson-7-in-zone.html). Writing from that zone, our most talented writers keep us glued to their books. But we have to wonder, how do they do "it"? Where do their minds take them so that they are able to keep us entranced in the spell of their fictional worlds?

Some of these award-winning storytellers have gifted us with memoirs in which they've attempted to explain answers to those questions. But most admit they cannot adequately explain how creativity happens. Here's what top-selling author Anne Lamott says in her memoir, *Bird by Bird*:

> You create these characters and figure out little by little what they say and do, but this all happens in a part of you to which you have no access—the unconscious. This is where the creating is done . . . you can't will yourself to be receptive. (Lamott 1994, 71–72)

Award-winning author Annie Dillard uses a house metaphor when she tries to explain the creative process:

> You hammer against the walls of your house. You tap the walls, lightly, everywhere. After giving years' attention to these things, you know what to listen for. (1989, 4)

And likewise, in Stephen King's memoir *On Writing*, he too suggests that his fiction comes from a zone he calls "a basement place . . . a far-seeing place" (King 2000, 95) where the "boys in the basement" reside (http://www.npr.org/ templates/story/story.php?storyid=1112273). So if even the best authors cannot explain how they compose their stories, is it any wonder we find fictional writing tough to teach?

In the poem "A Valentine for Ernest Mann," Naomi Shihab Nye (1994) suggests that "You can't order a poem like you order a taco" (70). I might add that you can't order creative writing or essays like a taco, either. I'll admit this is a bone I have to pick with those who expect and grade on-the-spot creativity. It's similar to expecting on-the-spot art, on-the-spot hoop shots, or an on-the-spot dance or music. So how do we solve this dilemma? Maybe the answer is to focus on text-based prompts when writing is being assessed (what some states have already done).

Text-Based Prompts

Most career writing is text-based. But text-based prompts are also found on school assessments in reading, math, science, and social studies. These prompts direct writers to seek out the facts, to go back to the text, to find exact information. As a consequence, text-based responses constructed by different writers often do not vary much in content—one of the key reasons why text-based assessments are easily electronically scored.

Where Are the Facts Located?

To further understand why text-based right answers on a test are so predict-ably similar, let's investigate a few text-based prompts. Here's an example of a text-based prompt from a reading assessment:

> At the end of the story, Betty and Juan throw down their books and cel-ebrate. Explain why they do this. What do their actions most likely mean for Zeth's future? Use details from the story to support your answer.

Students should understand that as soon as they see the words "use details from the story," they have very little freedom to express their own personal ideas. In some situations, the article or story may offer a few examples from which students are asked to select one or two. It is only those one or two right answers that offer a correct response. Therefore, correct text-based responses will not vary widely—unlike self-based responses.

Sometimes the text in a text-based prompt relates to facts from state stan-dards and curriculum, as the following facsimile of an elementary social studies prompt does.

> You've learned how important the Erie Canal was to many people living in the state of New York. Explain one advantage this waterway offered over other transportation sources.

Such fact-based prompts differ from those offered on most writing assess-ments, where open and creative thought is rewarded. Drop into creative writ-ing on most science tests and you'll no doubt shoot yourself in the foot. I became aware of students who did just that while I was correcting state assess-ments. I observed that many writers lost their way when they confused facts and fancy.

In the end, it all boils down to wiggle room. Every piece of writing allows a certain amount of wiggle room. Let's see why that is.

WIGGLE ROOM—OR NOT

Many students have trouble discerning how much freedom a composing task allows. Like some of today's reporters, responders can stray from the presented task, using more freedom than is allowed. How can we expect novices to understand the parameters of a writing task unless we immerse them in a grand variety—from the fact-focused to the cleverly creative?

Comparing Two Seemingly Similar Prompts

You can enter a conversation about wiggle room by offering students two similar prompts, but with one being more restrictive. For example, consider this reading prompt:

> Write four things that happen in the selection that change the way the street looks. Write them in the order that they happen in the selection.

It's obvious there is a right answer to this prompt. Not much room to wiggle, right?

But now read this writing prompt:

> Your school is planning field trips for the year. Write a letter to the principal telling her about an educational field trip you'd like to take. Be sure to give reasons why you've selected this place.

There are many right answers to this one, aren't there? Far more wiggle room and infinite right answers!

Appraising Wiggle Room

Some responses seem to be set in stone; there is no wiggle room. This means response possibilities are finite and writing boundaries are narrow. Yet other prompts have so many answer options that, conceivably, each student could compose a piece vastly different from anyone else's and still receive a high mark. Students need to understand this.

From my experience, the most effective, efficient way to drive this point home is to offer students a one-to-ten scale that locates writing with tons of wiggle room (very creative) on one side and writing with no wiggle room (very factual) on the other. One end designates few boundaries (from 1 to 5 on the scale); the other end has the tighter boundaries (from 5 to 10 on the scale).

Using the Boundaries Scale to Appraise Wiggle Room

Use the Boundaries Scale in Figure 1 (and on the CD and the book's appendix) for a quick, effective lesson on the latitude one has when composing any particular piece of writing. I begin by asking students where a letter to a friend might fall on the Boundaries Scale: "Talk to

Better Answer
Rubrics and Scales

your partner about where you'd put a letter to a friend on the scale. How much wiggle room do you have when you write to a friend?"

After the class has a chance to discuss this, I follow up with, "Now, hold up the number of fingers that indicates the place on this scale where you would put a letter to a friend." Next, I call on a few students to explain why they selected the number they did, but I don't indicate that any particular placement is right or wrong.

Instead, I move on to another kind of writing. "Okay," I say, "now suppose you are standing on that number that you gave for a *letter to a friend*. Point in the direction you would move for an *email to a friend*. Would you move to the left, the right, or would you stay put? Everybody, point!"

Again, I ask a few students to explain their decisions. But for emails to friends, most students tend to move in the same direction, which indicates that they are indeed beginning to understand some of the boundaries of writing. Even so, I continue offering more samples: a letter to a newspaper editor, a DVD manual, a response on a science test, your mom's memo to her boss. We've had some pretty interesting debates related to placement. Such disputes help to further solidify an understanding of writings' boundaries—and that is indeed the purpose of this activity.

Weave this activity into the curriculum all year. Use it for every prompt, as well as reading materials, all year long. Each time I use the activity, I suggest, "Think about where that piece of writing would fall on our scale. How much wiggle room do you (or did this author) have in constructing a response?"

Figure 1

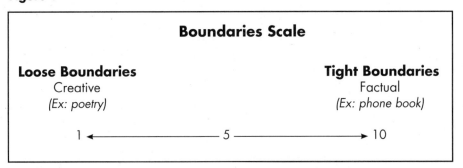

Some people write to entertain others, whereas others write to inform. Some combine the two. But many test correctors and employers do not want to be entertained. They want only information—correct information. That's why most prompts in reading, social studies, math, and science require creative *thinking,* but not creative *writing.* The younger the students, the more experiences they'll need in evaluating the differences between fact-focused and novelly nuanced prompts.

Graphing Real Writing

This activity helps connect students to writing in the real world. After students have had experience using the Boundaries Scale, they'll be better able to assess kinds of writing. So we ask them to interview their parents and others, investigating the kinds of writing they do in their careers: Are they writing stories? Memos? Persuasion pieces? Letters? How do they use writing in the real world? And how much wiggle room do they have?

After students have had time to gather this data, we make a real-world writing chart to show the prevalence of informative writing (text-based) and narrative/story-like writing (self-based) within our real-world lives. After everyone has had a chance to contribute, we can ask the students to partner and decide what the results show. (Most of us can predict that in our careers, we use informative writing far more than stories or narratives.)

After these experiences assessing various kinds of writing for the wiggle room they allow, students come to understand the boundaries they must consider as they construct responses to text-based and self-based prompts, as well as everything in between.

With this text-based/self-based consideration under our belts, we move on to the prompt's components.

THE COMPONENTS OF PROMPTS

Many of today's test prompts are full-blown tasks that remind me of memos I've received from my principal; directions that accompany grants; guidelines for publication submissions; and applications for schools and jobs. Yes, some of the prompts we're offering kids definitely possess real-world characteristics. And that's probably a good thing. It's just that our students haven't played this "game" before, so they need to understand all the rules and regulations in order to win. Why not begin by showing students all the pieces and parts to this new game, the components?

Prompts can possess one or more of the following three components:

The Three Components of Prompts
1. prompt background information
2. prompt petitions
3. prompt questions

After we show students how to analyze a prompt to locate these components, we can demonstrate strategies related to each. Let's begin with the background information component.

A Prompt's Background Information

Analyzing background information is no insignificant task, because information comes in many shapes and sizes, as well as a variety of locations. There may be a thick background section, a thin one, or no background information at all. Plus, some relevant information is inside the prompt, whereas other information is outside. What's more, relevant information can be presented in many forms: narrative, graph, chart, table, and others. Regardless, in order to construct a complete response, novices need experience in locating background information and in understanding its value. So let's investigate some characteristics of background information.

Background Information: Missing from Prompt
Some prompts are very short, offering the task in a mere sentence or two. They omit background information from the prompt itself. Look at this one, for instance:

> Explain how Anansi tricks Turtle.

Background Information: Inside the Prompt
On the other hand, background information frequently resides inside the prompt. More often than not, it precedes what the writer is asked or told to do. Here's an example:

> Joel worked hard to win the prize. He used his time wisely and focused on his goal. He also had the help of others. Think of a time when you reached an important goal. Explain how you reached your goal by comparing your struggles with Joel's.

Notice that the first three sentences provide background information, which the responder must keep in mind as he or she writes the response.

The final two sentences petition the writer in specific ways (the next section addresses these petitions).

Background Information: In a Variety of Forms

Background information is not always presented in a narrative form. Some prompts have pictorial information. Others contain relevant information in charts, graphs, and tables. Notice the chart reference in this prompt:

> Choose one of your favorite foods from the chart. Then use information from that chart to explain why you believe your choice is a healthy one.

> [Below this part of the prompt, readers find a detailed chart that they must use as a resource for their response.]

No doubt students who disregard the chart will veer from the path that leads to a better answer.

Background Information: Outside-the-Prompt References

Relevant facts also can be outside the prompt, though they are referenced inside. In order to weigh their importance, students must first find these facts—which brings us to an absolute: Responders *must* get into the habit of returning to a story they've just read, a piece of curriculum covered during the year, or even experiments or research done to uncover the details for their answer. Let's look at some examples.

Here's a prompt that refers the reader to prior course content, which becomes the location of a right answer:

> You've learned how the railway system changed life in this country. Explain one way that life was made better once Americans could travel by rail.

The following is a common return-to-text petition, but it refers the reader to what he or she just finished reading in order to locate necessary information (outside the prompt):

> Use details from the story to explain why flowers are so important to Muriel.

We might say that background information is all over the place—at least that's the way it probably looks to the kids. And that's exactly why we need to investigate many, many different kinds of prompts, considering each and every type and the placement of relevant information. Use the live links on the CD to locate a ton of examples from every curricular area.

Web Resources

Prewriting: 1.3

Prompt Petitions

We've all been petitioned, and most of us have signed petitions. Basically, *petitions are commands or imperatives*; they are terms that call us to act. They are one of the most important components of prompts, yet students tend to overlook them and their directive value. Why? Let's investigate.

Why Responders Overlook Petitions

Petitions get overlooked, because students are on another mission—a mission that focuses on questions and question marks. You see, we're all used to multiple-choice tests with all their questions, not petitions, so for decades our teacher mantra has been "Answer all the questions." But now on performance assessments, we must change that advice, because countless prompts contain more petitions than questions—and petitions end with a period. But it's tough to change our habits. So the next time you slip and say, "Answer all the questions" instead of "Respond to all the prompts," just stop for a second and tell the kids how tough it is to change that habit—and I guarantee, they'll help you remember and learn, themselves, in the process.

The habit of referring to "questions" is so engrained that even test makers goof sometimes. Documents on the website of the National Assessment of Educational Progress (NAEP) continue to refer to petitions as questions. Directions tell students to "Think carefully about each *question*" [my italics], but then, ironically, present them with a petition prompt: "Give an example from the article that shows Mandy was not a quitter" (National Center for Education Statistics 2007, 10). There is no question! See what I mean?

Nevertheless, there is a close relationship between questions and petitions—one that many novices don't understand. I tell students that petitions and questions are almost one and the same, and that petitions are *inside-out questions* and must, therefore, be treated as questions. However, they are not as easy to spot because they end with a period.

Real-World Examples Work Best

I reach for real-world examples when I introduce petitions. I tell the kids that every day we all receive petitions. Sometimes, moms and dads issue a petition, and at other times they use a question. I explain by using an entertaining entree—and one that I've found works for all ages. Students smile and connect when I ask, "How many of you have ever heard this prompt: 'Did you make your bed yet?' And when that question doesn't work, how many of you have heard this: 'Go make your bed!'" I guarantee the kids will connect. It's an entry point, a fun way to begin talking about the close connection between questions and petitions.

Petitions are those terms that tell us to explain, compare, describe, or discuss topics. Some interrogatives also weave their way into petitions. For instance, we might ask someone to "Explain *how* . . . " or "Discuss *why* . . . "

More than half the constructed-response tasks on state assessments now include petitions. Students who know about these inside-out questions prior to an assessment will not be misled by searching only for question marks. They'll simply turn petitions inside out.

For example, look at the following petition:

Explain how Little Red Riding Hood knew the wolf was not her grandmother.

For the sake of clarity and ease of use, we can invite students to change petitions such as this one to their interrogative form:

How did Little Red Riding Hood know the wolf was not her grandmother?

This also helps those who have difficulty with the part of Step 1 in the Better Answer protocol, which asks them to restate the question or petition. (Chapter 4 will explain Step 1 in more detail.) For some reason, kids find it easier to restate questions than petitions. So just show them how to turn those petitions into questions and all's well.

Petitions: Implicit or Explicit?

Responders need to understand that some petition terms, such as *write* or *explain*, indicate that it's time to put your pencil to the paper. I call these *explicit petitions*. Yet, there are some petitions that remind us only to think, and I call these *implicit petitions*. You can well imagine how the two kinds might confuse students, so mini-lessons related to the following explanations are very helpful.

Implicit Petitions Call Responders to Think

Implicit petitions are important because they focus our minds. They call on us to *think, remember, recall, consider, decide, imagine,* and *reflect*—all of which we do in our heads, even before we pick up our pencil. As students compose a response, however, they need to keep in mind the suggestions offered through the prompt's implicit petitions, much as they keep the background information in mind. As a matter of fact, I've had some students equate implicit petitions with background information, neither of which requires that we pick up our pencils.

Explicit Petitions Call Responders to Act

On the other hand, explicit petitions nudge us to pick up our pencils and act. Specific directives, such as *write, explain, tell, describe, compare, convince, identify, provide, use,* and *list* must receive our utmost attention. Ignore an explicit petition and the response definitely will suffer. So how might we tackle this implicit-explicit issue with students? The Petition Framework will help.

The Petition Framework

We know that each explicit petition possesses certain terms that point responders toward a better answer. In other words, petitions point us toward certain structures. I developed the Petition Framework (see Figure 2), which helps students understand how particular petitions lead quite naturally to related answer avenues or mind structures.

For example, when presented with a petition asking that they analyze, responders will have a head start if they know that they can begin with the framework of a list—one that is probably going to contain parts or steps. Consequently, their search for details is narrowed to a search for steps (key verbs) or a list of people, places, or events (key nouns). If a student is asked to compare, the Petition Framework will help them learn that a Venn diagram would be a useful prewriting tool. Many other petition terms are covered by the Petition Framework chart in Figure 2. How can we have students internalize all the facets of the Petition Framework? There are myriad ways, but let me share one activity that works well and complements the end of any unit of study.

Other Charts and Visuals

ACTIVITY

Using the Petition Framework

First, select a number of areas from your current unit of study that are necessary for its understanding and that are related to state standards. Then, present these important areas to the students. For instance, if the students are studying the Revolutionary War, some core concepts and understandings might be the manner in which the war began, those who fought in the war, the major battles, the reasons for the war, and so on. Because it is the end of the unit, students will possess related information; therefore, I ask partners to use those core areas to develop suitable petitions for each. This means they'll take pieces of core content (standards) to the Petition Framework, discuss the best match, and then develop a petition. As partners collaborate using the framework, they begin to internalize its structure.

Figure 2

The Petition Framework

Key Petition Terms	Meaning	Framework	Examples
Analyze (common with why and how)	Separate into its parts.	An ordered list framework containing parts or steps	Analyze the personality of the main character.
Compare	Examine, noting similarities and differences.	Venn diagram to show differences of each with likeness in the center	Compare two ways of doing something.
Contrast	Examine, noting the differences only.	T-chart (two columns below a heading) to contrast left to right	Contrast two or more approaches.
Define	State a precise meaning or the basic qualities of something.	An ordered list or outline framework	Define the term used.
Discuss (common with why and how)	Present background information with supporting or descriptive details.	T-chart with important factors on left, details on right	Discuss the minor events leading to a major event.
Describe (common with why and how)	Convey an idea, qualities, or background information.	Semantic web: subject in middle, surrounded by numbered qualities	Describe a person, place, thing, or event.
Evaluate	Place judgment, but support using details.	T-chart listing pros next to cons	Evaluate the actions, behaviors, or decisions of individuals or groups.
Explain (common with how and why)	Make clear or offer reason.	T-chart listing facts and supportive details	Explain an action or how/why something happened.
Give/provide	Offer facts related to topic.	T-chart using facts and supportive details	Give several reasons, examples, possibilities, alternatives.
Review	Examine major elements again, sometimes using a critical perspective.	Outline or list framework	Review paths followed, steps taken, important events.
Tell (common with how and why)	Offer facts related to topic.	T-chart using facts and supportive details	Give several reasons, examples, possibilities, alternatives.
Use	Do the task in a specific manner.	Outline or list framework	Use details or information to support.
Write	Usually use as a prompt for a specific task.	Outline or list framework	Write: about; telling; explaining; describing.

Students in fourth grade developed petitions that looked like this:

- Tell what started the war.
- Describe the food they ate.
- List what they used to fight.
- Explain how they got ready to fight.
- Compare how things were different before and after the war.

Great prompts, right? So why not use the students' collection of petitions as a resource for your actual unit assessment? Students might even be excited about taking that test!

A Prompt's Questions

Now that we've discussed the less familiar components of a prompt, we can touch on the most familiar: *questions*—those parts of a prompt that we know by the punctuation mark at the end. But we also know questions by their many interrogative terms, which usually introduce them and often begin with a *wh-*.

Students are well aware of the most common interrogatives, but they are astounded when presented with the entire Better Questions Menu shown in Figure 3, which sports every conceivable interrogative possibility. Sixty-four different interrogative types! Sure, this list will help teachers develop assessments; but believe it or not, when presented with this grand variety, students actually have fun discovering the myriad ways to state a question. As they observe the patterns in the groupings, they come to understand the way in which certain terms will direct them toward a better answer.

Figure 3

Prewriting: 1.4

Other Charts and Visuals

Better Questions Menu

Who is . . .	*When should . . .*	*How will . . .*	*Why can . . .*
Who was . . .	*When could . . .*	*How might . . .*	*Why does . . .*
Who can . . .	*Where is . . .*	*How should . . .*	*Why did . . .*
Who does . . .	*Where was . . .*	*How could . . .*	*Why will . . .*
Who did . . .	*Where can . . .*	*What is . . .*	*Why might . . .*
Who will . . .	*Where does . . .*	*What was . . .*	*Why should . . .*
Who might . . .	*Where did . . .*	*What can . . .*	*Why could . . .*
Who should . . .	*Where will . . .*	*What does . . .*	*Which is . . .*
Who could . . .	*Where might . . .*	*What did . . .*	*Which was . . .*
When is . . .	*Where should . . .*	*What will . . .*	*Which can . . .*
When was . . .	*Where could . . .*	*What might . . .*	*Which does . . .*
When can . . .	*How is . . .*	*What should . . .*	*Which did . . .*
When does . . .	*How was . . .*	*What could . . .*	*Which will . . .*
When did . . .	*How can . . .*	*What if . . .*	*Which might . . .*
When will . . .	*How does . . .*	*Why is . . .*	*Which should . . .*
When might . . .	*How did . . .*	*Why was . . .*	*Which could . . .*

Thick or Thin: Length Matters

Some question terms prompt a more in-depth, rich response, whereas others call for a brief, surface response. For instance, *why, how,* and *might* questions or petitions generally call for some in-depth searching and connecting. They tend to evoke deep, rich responses that require more paper space to answer. Harvey and Goudvis (2007) call these "thick" responses.

Questions that focus on *who, where,* and *when* often call for less lengthy, easily located, surface details. Harvey and Goudvis call the responses to such prompts "thin."

I take the concept a step further by dubbing prompts themselves thick or thin. In other words, the term *who* usually elicits a brief response and would therefore be called a thin prompt.

Thin Prompts

Thin questions and petitions are frequently literal and evoke surface-level answers that can usually be located right there in the observable text. They can readily be evidenced as right or wrong, as well as easily corrected. When? On December 12, 1942. Where? In northern Italy. I tell the kids this so they won't spend an inordinate amount of time collecting a bushel of details to answer a thin question, especially when thick questions lie in wait. I know students fall prey to this because when I was a corrector for the state performance assessments, I noticed that many students spent too much time on thin questions and then paid for it later when they lacked the time to answer a thick one. We can help kids predict the prompts whose responses will require their greatest efforts so they do not misplace time and energy.

Thick Prompts

On the other hand, thick prompts that incorporate terms like *why* and *how* are of a different nature, provoking interesting, exciting, and sometimes debatable answers. They require more explanation, more details, more evidence. They call to our deep structure (Chomsky 2008), requiring us to crawl down between the lines, revisit prior text and relevant information, and make subtle connections between what the text is saying and what our experiences suggest. Such responses may require a grand search, and as a consequence, thick prompts require far more time to answer.

It therefore makes sense to teach students the differences between thin and thick prompts. Invite them to investigate by trying the questions and petitions on for size. Support them in prompt development by providing opportunities that put them in the driver's seat. Only by exploring a variety of prompts—each one as a whole—will they come to understand the predictable differences in their parts.

In Search of Thick and Thin

A simple sorting activity can help students begin to distinguish the depth of questions and expected answers. In this activity we provide partners with a sheet of questions from the Better Questions Menu, which they cut apart and then place under the related heading: Thick or Thin.

Obviously, this provokes some conversation and maybe even some debates. But this is what we want. We want kids comparing thick and thin questions, understanding question commonalities and differences, and climbing into the depths of a culture of inquiry. This activity can serve only as the tip of the interrogative iceberg.

Why is this important? It's important because developing deep, rich answers for the thick questions is a school assessment skill, but it is also a real-life career skill. When the supervisor asks a thick question like "Why are sales down?" it's probably not wise to answer with a thin response such as "People are not buying." That supervisor, no doubt, wants to know every single detail related to why sales are down, so that the company can do something about it. "People are not buying" is an answer, but it is a gist, or general, answer. It is a surface-structure answer. The boss wants the details to back it up.

Considering Question Attributes

After students have a background in thick and thin questions, we can move on to other question categories—categories that will help them capably spot relevant details. Most adults realize that when a question begins with *who*, its answer probably involves a person or people. Likewise, *when* relates to time and *where* to place. As students come to understand such relationships, they become more capable of skimming and scanning material for specific information. The Question Connections chart lists some types of connections along the top horizontal axis.

Struggling readers tend to use the same strategy for every question; that is, they start at the beginning of the referenced piece and read straight through until they come to the answer. These students benefit from lots of experience matching *who* questions with people and *where* questions with places.

An obvious strategy would be to have students locate the in-text answers for each specific question type, help them skim for specific details, and show them how to search for the capital letters related to important places and people. All that is well and good, and it does help, but I suggest that we turn the

Other Charts and Visuals

ownership around; let the students develop the related questions from their content material. They will internalize the process when they, themselves, must search for the context and the details in order to compose the question—just as we teachers do when we construct their tests.

Turning the Tables: Students Develop the Prompts

Other Charts and Visuals

As a review or reinforcement for necessary content concepts, as well as to support those question-answer codependent relationships, we can invite the students themselves into the prompt construction process. Use the Question Connections chart from the CD to support this activity.

To begin, invite partners to develop one important question (relevant to a current unit of study) for each of the following categories:
time
place
people
past
present
future

Then, invite each dyad to trade their questions with another pair of students. Both pairs will be expected to use the Better Answer protocol to respond to some of those questions. Afterward, each pair can pass its answers back to the questions' authors instead of the teacher. The creators of the questions can easily correct the answers since they developed the questions out of the answers in the first place. In this kind of back-and-forth activity, the codependency of questions and answers becomes evident. Furthermore, it makes an interesting way to study content.

Marking the Contents of Prompts

I like to get kids in the groove of dissecting prompts to identify their background information, petitions, and questions. To encourage this, I ask partners to share and discuss a page containing several prompts. After they discuss its contents, I suggest they take turns underlining all the background information and circling both petitions and questions.

Afterward, they can go back through and put a star beside the explicit petitions they must address in writing.

I find that getting students into this habit helps them better analyze every prompt they meet. Ideally, your students are allowed to mark their test booklets. If not, at least their minds will still analyze the prompt into its significant parts, causing petitions and questions to stand out as though circled.

CREATING GOOD PROMPTS

It's easy to see how the information in this chapter, along with the related strategies, will help students in constructing sound responses. But what's more, understanding prompts in this way helps *teachers* when they need to construct a prompt. Teachers who read this chapter develop classroom assessments in a more informed manner. They understand what can be included in a prompt and then make choices related to those possibilities. And as they do this, they prepare their students for all kinds of prompts—on tests and in the real world.

IN THE END

Lessons related to prompts are fun and easy. They should not consume precious hours of instructional time. It's a relief to know that the minimal amount of time it takes to introduce these concepts and strategies pays off many times over when students begin to construct responses, because they know where they are going and what they must do. They understand, as ancient poet Rumi did, that "The answer is *inside* the question."

PART 2

WRITING:
CONSTRUCTING
A RESPONSE

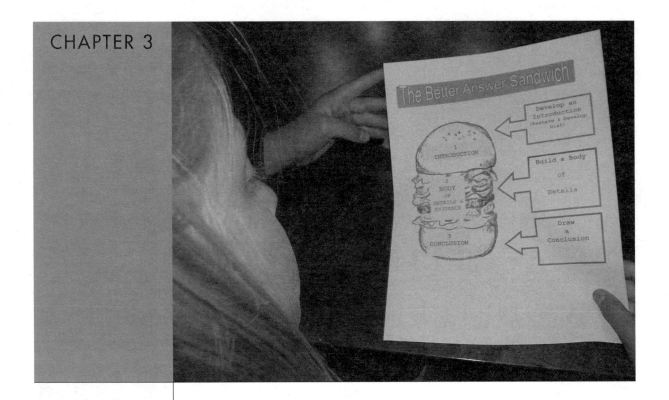

CHAPTER 3

GETTING STARTED WITH THE BETTER ANSWER PROTOCOL

*Stylistic imitation is one thing, a perfectly honorable way to get started
as a writer (and impossible to avoid, really; some sort of imitation
marks each new stage of a writer's development).*
—Stephen King, *On Writing: A Memoir of the Craft*

By grade 8, most students have had considerable experience reading and writing creative pieces, many of which derive from stories and personal experiences, whose purpose is entertainment. They've had plenty of instruction in journal writing, memoirs, narratives, and poetry. Yet, how many have been afforded instruction in more structured writing—the kind that's found at the other end of the Boundaries Scale? Or the kind they'll need in their careers?

School tests, as well as job-related writing, usually call for more structured writing—writing whose purpose is to inform. On subject-area tests and in most careers, students write primarily to present information, not to entertain—and the more expeditiously they can do this, the better. Enter the Better Answer protocol.

Before we teach kids how to write a structured essay or response using the Better Answer protocol, we should show them what this kind of writing looks like. Novices need a comprehensive knowledge of response genres before we ask them to mimic what they've witnessed.

EXEMPLARS AND MENTOR TEXTS

Probably one of the single most important ways you can help students become better response writers is by sharing with them responses of every shade and hue. We call the best of these pieces of writing *exemplars* or *mentor texts*—texts we want our students to mimic. In his memoir, Stephen King tells how, for him, "imitation preceded creation." He says, "I would copy *Combat Casey* comics word for word in my Blue Horse tablet, sometimes adding my own descriptions where they seemed appropriate" (2000, 14). *Combat Casey* was his mentor text until King's mom told him to try writing one of his own.

What about our own writing mentors? I know that when I want to place an ad in the newspaper, I turn to existing ads. I mimic the structure of the best ones—maybe even their wording. In other words, we writers use masterful models *before* we enter the task ourselves.

That's why students need to read and analyze tons of responses. It allows them a window into success. Furthermore, it's helpful to discuss ways they'd turn poor responses into better ones. Many states now offer response examples from various levels of expertise, and these can be used for classroom demonstration purposes. Check the CD's Resources section for live links to state exemplars. But also investigate links to sites with real-world exemplars. Some of the best constructed responses come from environmental organizations who enlist professionals to construct petitions—as in "sign this petition." These documents can offer a sound example, one that usually elevates student interest.

So just as Part I on prewriting emphasized the importance of analyzing a plethora of prompts, I now suggest we offer students a wide range of responses. And let's do it *before* Step 1 in the response writing process, so they know what a response looks like and sounds like *before* being expected to construct one.

LOOKING GOOD, SOUNDING SMART!

I tell my students to mimic those mentor texts—at least until they get the hang of the genre. It's a way to sound smart. After all, if Stephen King did it, why shouldn't we?

But there's another way to sound smart: Just follow the lead of the prompt. Certainly test manufacturers expect responders to stick to the given prompt. Real life, too, offers up numerous times when following the prompt is the best advice. And that's exactly why Step 1 tells responders to restate the question or petition. It's a way to sound smart.

I also repeatedly remind students that *first impressions count*, so when we're writing for someone else—someone who will judge our work—it's not only important to sound smart, we must look smart. Why? For the same reasons I wouldn't wear ragged jeans to an interview. When an assessor picks up my paper, I want that person to think, "Hmm, this person's paper looks very neat and well organized. I bet she's smart!"

Writing: II.10, II.11

Better Answer
Sandwich Charts

Single or Multiple Paragraphs?

I mentioned earlier that prompts and responses come in every size and shape, so before we begin Step 1, let me say that the emphasis of Chapters 4, 5, and 6 in Part II of this book is the construction of *one-paragraph responses*. Nevertheless, at the end of Chapter 6 and on the CD, I offer some handy ideas, visuals, and lesson plans for converting a one-paragraph response into multiple paragraphs.

Does the Response Make Sense **Without** the Prompt?

Students often write as if the teacher *already knows* the answer (and of course, he or she does). Basically, such novices do not as yet understand how to play this new kind of "game," where, even though the teacher knows the answer, responders must still look good and sound smart by writing to the prompt, not to the teacher.

For responses that require one or more paragraphs, a key to sounding smart is imbedded in this simple idea: *The response should make sense even without reading the prompt.* In other words, if we handed a stranger the response, would it make sense, or would he or she need the prompt too? The smartest sounding responses can stand alone.

More about this later, but for now, please know that the Better Answer protocol leads students toward stand-alone, meaningful responses. Therefore, once they build an answer using this structure, their responses not only will make sense independent of the prompt, they will also look good and sound smart. And it is the Better Answer Sandwich that will lead them to success.

Figure 4

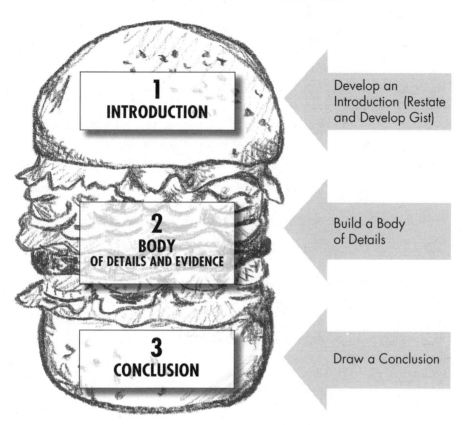

The Better Answer Sandwich

1
INTRODUCTION

Develop an
Introduction (Restate
and Develop Gist)

2
BODY
OF DETAILS AND EVIDENCE

Build a Body
of Details

3
CONCLUSION

Draw a Conclusion

THE ANSWER SANDWICH: A VISUAL SUPPORT STRUCTURE

Teachers and students find the Better Answer Sandwich a very effective tool—a reliable crutch that makes an abstract process more concrete. That's why I place this sound and memorable structure here, *before* describing the Better Answer process itself.

We'll use this sandwich structure throughout the book, but I'll begin by modeling its use through interesting personal prompts (self-based) and prompts related to easy fairy tales (text-based). I first demonstrate with a think-aloud, and then gradually invite the students into the process and eventually into autonomy. This *gradual release method* is the basic instructional sequence used throughout this book.

Better Answer
Sandwich Charts

I invite you to copy the Better Answer Sandwich from the CD. Transfer it onto a chart that has been laminated with plastic so it can be reused. (If your school's copier will not accommodate this, most large office stores will.)

Once I have the chart posted where students can see it, I discuss the three parts of the sandwich, suggesting to the group that the top bun (Step 1) and the bottom bun (Step 3) are very similar—just like a real sandwich. The middle section (Step 2) has several layers (all the different details and evidence)—also just like a real sandwich.

Another real-sandwich quality relates to this graphic's ordered layers; that is, in a real sandwich, peanut butter goes on before jelly, mayonnaise before lettuce. The Answer Sandwich also has a particular order, which will be thoroughly described in Chapters 4, 5, and 6. But for now, let's take a quick peek at the top, middle, and bottom.

Top Bun of Sandwich: An Introduction

The top bun holds Step 1, the introduction to the response. It includes (1) a restatement of the prompt's explicit questions and/or petitions and (2) a gist (or general) answer. Chapter 4 describes this step in detail. Once Step 1 is complete, writers will have constructed the main idea for their response. Following its direction, they'll move on to the evidence that supports that main idea.

The Sandwich Middle: A Body of Details

The middle section of the sandwich holds a body of details (or evidence) that support the gist answer. It is Step 2 of the Better Answer protocol. Collecting facts, organizing data, using transitions, and several other tasks related to constructing evidence are incorporated into this step's lessons, which again use gradual release methodology. Step 2 is the focus of Chapter 5. When the middle of the sandwich is complete, we move on to the bottom bun, the concluding statement.

The Bottom Bun: A Conclusion

When I introduce Step 3 to students, I suggest that they can simply create a kind of restatement of the introduction (or top bun). Our primary task in the conclusion is just to offer a sense of finality to the piece. If the writer is talented enough to shade and hue that concluding statement with a bit of voice, a touch of humor, well, then, so much the better.

Don't Forget About the **Better Answers** CD

Remember that the CD offers not only all of the visuals included in this book, but also lesson plans, related web links, and other helpful items—even PowerPoint slides for use in lessons. Therefore, while reading Part II, keep in mind that the CD contains everything you need to effectively carry what's in this book into your classroom. The first edition of *Better Answers* did not contain a CD. I hope its inclusion allows for a bit more R and R in your life.

Another Reminder: Do a Baseline Assessment

If you haven't already, now's the time to copy one of the CD's fairy tales or fables along with one of the suggested prompts, and ask students to respond. You'll then have *preinstruction data*. So *before* you move into the Better Answer protocol, read a tale, then have each student construct a response. This will serve as your baseline assessment. Don't even worry about marking the papers, but it's wise to examine them a bit for a basic overview.

The primary reason for this preassessment is to validate growth once the results of the post-test are in. That is, you can compare that preassessment data with the postassessment data *after* you teach the protocol—evidence of your successful instruction as well as evidence for your students' response growth.

I've done this with many classes, and each time I can scarcely believe the progress students make between the pre- and postassessment. You'll feel like shaking each student's hand. And maybe you should!

The Better Answer Protocol: A Versatile Tool

Teachers always tell me tales about how this protocol has not only helped their students, but also helped the teachers themselves in their own writing worlds. In other words, this is not just a school tool. It's a life tool—one that not only helps our kids, but also supports adult response-writers. Try the protocol out the next time you receive an important prompt, and then, when someone asks, "Who needs it?" I bet you'll answer, "Everyone!"

CHAPTER 4

DEVELOP AN
INTRODUCTION

"Where shall I begin, please Majesty?" he asked.
"Begin at the beginning,"
the King said gravely.
—Lewis Carroll, *Alice's Adventures in Wonderland*

It is obvious to most of us that an introduction comes at the beginning of anything. And although we adults may not need an introduction to the general
purpose of an introduction, many of our students may. For example, we could
revisit introductions to new people, recent movies (trailers), books, unfamiliar
foods, or a new neighborhood. Afterward, with this broader perspective in
mind, students can move more specifically into the purpose for constructing
an introduction to a response.

Before I dig into strategies related to Step 1, I always take out the Better Answer Sandwich chart and quickly review the three sandwich parts. That way, students see the whole before we fragment it into its parts. With that in mind, we can move forward into the first part of Step 1: Restate the question or petition.

Writing: II.1, II.2

PART 1 IN THE TOP BUN: RESTATE THE QUESTION OR PETITION

Step 1 begins with restating the prompt's question or petition. It happens to be the easiest part of the process, but it's also probably the most important piece, because it directs the responder toward the right path—not just in school, but also in real life. People use restating in their jobs, during interviews, or anytime they want to align with the purpose behind the prompt.

Restating also makes people sound smart and articulate. Not long ago I was listening to *Talk of the Nation*'s *Science Friday* on National Public Radio. Ira Flatow was interviewing a notable scientist, and each time he asked that scientist a question, the scientist began his answer by restating the interviewer's question. He restated it every time! This is something that good communicators do in real life, especially when they want to look good and sound smart. And that is exactly what I tell students.

RESTATING: A PORTAL TO THE ANSWER

Restating also becomes a portal to the answer; it leads the student more naturally toward the next step, which is the answer. I noticed when I surveyed grade 4 students' brief and extended responses from their state assessments that many times they did not have the correct answer because *they did not appear to know what the question was*. It often sounded like the writer was beginning in the middle of nowhere, and although he was somewhere, it was not usually where the answer was. But when responders begin with a restatement that uses the question's words, it locates them exactly where they should be.

This is why I begin with restating and consider it a fundamental step in the process. Once this step is in place, the next unfolds quite naturally.

INSTRUCTIONAL STRATEGIES FOR RESTATING

Using Color for Sandwich Parts

I use different colors to emphasize each section of a response—green (a get-going color) for the top bun, or introduction, blue for the middle layers, or details, and red (the stop color) for the bottom bun, or conclusion. Color is always motivational, and besides, kids love to use colored pencils and markers. So take out your green marker for Step 1, and let's get started.

Modeling That Uses Personal Questions

I begin Step 1 by discussing what it means to restate a question, but I soften the process by using personal, self-based prompts, rather than text-based. Obviously, kids are more interested in our personal matters. Plus, this approach keeps meaning front and center within a modeling process. For instance, I often show students how to restate the question, "What do you do in the evening when you get home from school?"

One word of caution when constructing those first demonstration questions: Make certain your example is a thick question—the kind of question that calls for a rich response. We're trying to avoid yes and no answers, because we will use these same prompts again in Steps 2 and 3 of the protocol. It's also wise to save all the restatement charts developed during this first step. Not only will they serve as anchors, but they eliminate rewriting as you move into Steps 2 and 3.

To lay the groundwork, I restate several questions and petitions. Here are some self-based examples of questions and petitions that work well:

- What do you do in the evening when you get home from school?
- Explain why it is important to be on time for school every day.
- How do the members of your family enjoy free time together?
- Describe what people do to take good care of their pets.
- How would you change our school, if it were possible?

OPEN-ENDED RESTATEMENTS

It's important to note that restating can be done in two forms: open-ended and closed. *Open-ended restatements* end without closure and usually with a transition term such as *because*. Selecting from the personal prompts just listed, I model a couple of open-ended restatements for the students, and then invite them into the process. (I teach closed restatements later in Step 1, after students understand gist answers.) This beginning part is all oral, and we do not at this time move on to the answer.

Our open restatements for the preceding questions and petitions might be worded as follows:

Open Restatements
- In the evening when I get home from school, I . . . *(no transition term)*
- It is important to be on time for school every day because . . . *(contains transition because)*

- The members of my family enjoy free time together by . . . *(contains transition by)*
- To take care of their pets, people . . . *(no transition)*
- If I did not know a friend's phone number, I would . . . *(no transition)*

After we've played with multiple restatement versions of a variety of questions orally, we move into the written mode.

HOW TO DEVELOP A SELF-BASED RESTATEMENT

I initially demonstrate how it helps to mark off the question's words as they are used in the restatement. We can then scribe from those words to develop our restatement.

For example, after placing the first question (What do you do in the evening when you get home from school?) on the chart, I demonstrate how the idea works. As I restate the question, I underline the words that I restate, crossing out words and writing substitutions above the crossed-out words:

What do ~~you~~ do <u>in</u> <u>the</u> <u>evening</u> <u>when</u> ~~you~~ <u>get</u> <u>home</u> <u>from</u> <u>school</u>?

In the evening when I get home from school, I . . .

Pronoun Substitution in Self-Based Responses

Pronoun substitutions frequently occur when restating self-based prompts. Most pronouns must be changed to have the writing make sense and sound syntactically acceptable. For example, *What did you do last weekend?* becomes *Last weekend I . . .* rather than *Last weekend you . . .* I find that this crossing out and substituting when modeling is especially important for ESL and special education students, who might not readily make such changes.

I make it very clear that I think it's important to incorporate as many of the words in the question as possible. Students who use only a few of the question's words often construct answers that are slightly or completely off-base. Therefore, we work hard to get as many of those words in our restatements as possible.

Verb Tense May Change

Verb tense, too, sometimes changes in the restatement of both text- and self-based responses. Again, I slash and overwrite to show students how I change a verb's tense to make it sound right. For instance, in the following sentence I substituted *thought* for *think* by crossing out *think* and writing *thought* above it.

<pre>   thought
Why did <u>the</u> <u>wicked</u> <u>stepmother</u> ~~think~~ <u>Snow</u> <u>White</u> <u>was</u> <u>still</u> <u>alive</u>?</pre>

The wicked stepmother thought Snow White was still alive because . . .

And I do call these words just what they are: *verbs*. By combining discussions related to pronoun and verb substitutions within ongoing anchor demonstrations, meanings are rehearsed again and again.

Scribing the Restatement

After I have completed the oral restatement and the marking of the original prompt on the chart, I scribe that restatement below the prompt on the chart. When scribing restatements, it's wise to keep each different prompt's introductory sentence, or partial sentence, on a separate chart or transparency so that when you move on to Steps 2 and 3, you can return to these previously composed restatements. This eliminates redoing previous sections each time. It also serves as a ready and observable review or anchor for Step 1.

Another element that works well when incorporated into an open-ended restatement is the ellipsis, the three sequenced dots that mean more is to come. Because we are not yet completing the restatement sentence with its gist answer, but instead leaving it open, the ellipsis becomes a perfect placeholder. I might warn, however, that many students develop a love affair with those three little dots and want to leave them there—even after the rest of the sentence has been constructed! Yet, ellipses serve their purpose well, for each ellipsis becomes a concrete "ta-da-a-a-a" fanfare as it calls forth the answer.

The Students' Turn to Restate Using Words from the Prompt

After modeling once or twice, I invite the students to come up and do the underlining, the slashing, and the substituting, as their classmates offer restatement suggestions for each chart's prompt. When it's their turn to try out the process, I make a really big deal out of students whose restatements use almost every word in the question.

Basically, it's important for students to know that there is more than one right way to word an answer on a performance assessment. So I extend multiple invitations to restate the same question in different ways. Such second and third versions can be scribed in another location so that the chart remains open for the selected restatement, ready to be reused during future demonstrations of Steps 2 and 3.

HOW TO DEVELOP A TEXT-BASED RESTATEMENT

When students have a little experience developing self-based restatements, we easily slide into text-based prompts and their restatements. But as we do this, we move across the Boundaries Scale and watch how our response choices narrow.

I always begin text-related prompts using well-known fairy tales and fables and prepare the students for the experience by first reading to them a brief version of a tale, then afterward visiting its prompt. Before the lesson, I place each of these prompts on a separate transparency or chart page, leaving room for the answers that will be developed in the course of the protocol lessons. These separate transparencies or charts become anchor charts.

Select a tale or fable, along with a prompt. Just as we did for self-based prompt restatement, underline the words that will become part of the restatement. For example, we can use "Goldilocks and the Three Bears" and do the following:

> *Prompt:* Why <u>were</u> <u>the</u> <u>three</u> <u>bears</u> <u>upset</u> <u>when</u> <u>they</u> <u>got</u> <u>home</u> <u>from</u> <u>their</u> <u>walk</u>?

> *Response:* The three bears were upset when they got home from their walk because . . .

Note the lack of pronoun and verb substitutions in this example. This is often the case in text-based restatements. With these teacher-led practice experiences under their belts, students are ready to collaborate with a partner in constructing other text-based restatements. I read a short tale, after which I distribute a few questions to each dyad. Partners then "share the pen" as they take turns restating, marking, and scribing their restatements. Observing and supporting, I cruise the class as they work. Later, in a whole-class setting, we decide on a favorite restatement for each prompt.

No Noun Substitutions

When restating text-based prompts, exact word match keeps responders focused in the right direction, but it also allows the response to stand alone and make sense without the prompt—to sound smart. Responders should stick to exact word match on nouns, bypassing a common practice among students of replacing nouns with pronouns. Responders who substitute pronouns for nouns confuse those who read the response. For instance, if we asked, *Why did the wicked stepmother think Snow White was still alive?* it is common practice for students to develop restatements such as: *She thought she was still alive because* . . . When finished, this response could not stand alone, because without the prompt, the reader does not know who the two *shes* are. This is especially relevant in text-based responses. I use a memorable visual to aid this process.

To discourage replacement of nouns in introductory sentences, I make a large chart of the most common (subjective) pronouns. Then I put a slash across the chart, similar to the "No smoking" sign. It looks like this:

Reading a couple of ill-constructed introductions usually drives the point home. But issues such as this one also demonstrate the need to discern text-based from self-based responses.

A Spotlight on Transitional Terms

Now that I've mentioned nouns, pronouns, and verbs, I'd like to draw attention to the transitions that connect the restatement to the gist. Call them transitions or call them conjunctions, the roots of both terms lead us to their purpose. They are important because, serving as connectors, they usher us directly into the gist.

I've developed a list of sample text-based restatements with their prompts. I show here how you can highlight transitions to demonstrate variety. I like to underline or highlight the transitions we incorporate, so that students become familiar with the options. Some past examples included the following:

Better Answer
Transitions Charts

Restatement Transitions
- Why wasn't Little Red Riding Hood afraid of the wolf? Little Red Riding Hood was not afraid of the wolf <u>because</u> . . .
- Why did the wolf run to Grandmother's house?
  The wolf ran to Grandmother's house <u>to</u> . . .
- Explain how Father got rid of the wolf.
  Father got rid of the wolf <u>by</u> . . .
- When was Little Red Riding Hood afraid?
  Little Red Riding Hood was afraid <u>when</u> . . .
- Tell how Little Red Riding Hood might not have been bothered by the wolf.
  Little Red Riding Hood might not have been bothered by the wolf <u>if</u> . . .

As the Better Answer process develops, students begin to feel the connections existing between response transitions and prompt terms. They realize that *because* often follows *why* and that *by* follows *how*, all of which again helps lead responders to a better answer.

Integrating Restating Throughout the Day

For some students, particularly novices, it's necessary to use several fairy tales and provide numerous restating experiences; however, most kids quickly understand how to use this first step. As a matter of fact, they enjoy transferring it into other areas of the curriculum, so that if we encounter questions in science or social studies, I might say, "Hey! Let's try to restate these questions as we answer them." To the students, restating quickly becomes the easy part. And that is just how we want them to feel!

ACTIVITY

Who's Using Restatements?

It's fun to take the lead from the scientist interviewed on NPR. Students need to see how important people really do restate; it's a life skill. Therefore, we ask them to listen online to NPR.org or PBS.org to locate interviews (especially on *Science Friday* or *Talk of the Nation*) where restating is common. Students love this because it takes on the air of a scavenger hunt. It's also interesting to note how critical they can be as they notice instances where restatements were not used, but should have been.

Once some sample interviews are found, transcripts of taped recordings or podcasts can be collected and shared with classmates. They can also become part of next year's examples.

ASSESSING ♦ CONFERRING

ASSESSMENT TYPE: **Observation During Partner Activities**

FOCUS QUESTIONS

♦ Did you use most of the words?
♦ Did you reread your writing? (Read it to me.)
♦ Does your spelling match the question's?
♦ Did you use a transition word? Which one?
♦ Did you have to substitute for any pronouns or verbs? Which ones?
♦ Were you restating a question or a petition?

Restating Old Test Questions

Another idea gathers its momentum from the formal assessment world. I offer actual (previously used and released) test questions for the students to restate. (This book's CD contains live links that will lead you directly to state assessment examples.) If your students are like our students, they will respond, "You mean these were real test questions!?" And their gestures show they are suddenly more engaged.

I save these test questions to use during a paired-partner collaboration, but I always model the first restatement for them, following the same procedure as for prior modeling. The group tends to stay more engaged when they know that we are working with what was once "the real thing." As we proceed, I keep hoping that they are thinking, "That restating we did with fairy tales was a piece of cake—and this doesn't seem much different. Hey! I can do this!"

The simplistic beginning to Step 1, practicing restatements, steers students right into the other half of this step: developing a gist answer. At first, this may seem somewhat more intimidating, because it would appear that we are actually completing the response. This is not so; in this step we seek only the general, or gist, answer, not the entire answer. Let's investigate the process.

PART 2 OF THE TOP BUN: DEVELOP A GIST ANSWER

While assessing hundreds of responses, I noticed that most of the time when students did not incorporate enough evidence or details in their responses, it was because they had answered the test question superficially; they included only a couple of supportive details—a wee morsel of an answer—and then said, "That's that! I'm finished!"

In reaction to these minimally detailed answers, I decided to approach this part of the process using a minimalist perspective. "If ya can't beat 'em, join 'em." And that is exactly what I did. I asked the students to develop an answer that included no details at all. A *gist answer would be only a clue to the whole answer*, the gist of it. It would hint at it, but not provide detailed information. In so doing, students would create an introductory statement that was so general, it would beg for details to back it up. And, it worked!

What Is a Gist Answer?

A key point that we want students to understand is that a gist answer should not be confused with the detailed answer. As a matter of fact, I begin by telling them, "A gist answer should have no details."

"So why use it?" they ask.

"The restatement and the gist answer are there to introduce the paragraph's topic or the detailed answer," I respond. So a gist statement in a single-paragraph response contains *no important details*—only the *main idea* of the response. It's a very *general answer*. Some might call it the *topic sentence* or the *thesis statement*. It offers us only the gist of the whole answer. And we'll know a gist answer because it makes us want to ask its author, "What do you mean?" In other words, rather than satisfy the prompt, the gist should just provoke more questions: How do you know that? Where's your evidence? What do you mean?

Wedded to the restatement, this gist answer is what our teachers always told us about how good essay paragraphs begin. Most well-constructed expository paragraphs begin with a main idea. Essentially, once we complete all of Step 1, we will have constructed the main idea for our response.

GOOD AND POOR SELF-BASED GISTS

One way to develop skill and understanding of this part of the process is to show students some of the unacceptable, overly detailed answers, which might look correct, followed by acceptable gist answers. Let me provide some examples related to our first self-based anchor, which we created earlier. We reread the prompt and our restatement from our anchor chart. Then, we mull over the following restatements and answers, which sound somewhat correct, but are unacceptable because they include too much. They offer too few details for a full answer, yet too many for a gist answer.

Demonstrating Poor Self-Based Gists

I move away from our anchor to a separate chart that contains the following non-gist answers to our question:

Restatement with Poor Self-Based Gists

Prompt: What do you do in the evening when you get home from school?
Examples of Poor Gists:
- In the evening when I get home from school, I watch TV, make dinner, and relax before bedtime.
- In the evening when I get home from school, I am tired so I do not make supper until I've rested a bit.
- In the evening when I get home from school, the first thing I do is walk the dog on the beach.

We investigate that first nongist answer, discussing why it is not a gist answer: "This first answer is dotted with details, yet it does not introduce what's to come. It sells my answer short," I explain. "It's too early in the paragraph to present all these details." Then I take my marker and highlight *watch TV*, *make dinner*, and *relax before bedtime*. "No details in a gist answer," I remind the students as I slash out details.

We go on and do the others in the same manner, but the students participate in the highlighting and the reasoning. When we finish, it is time to move into acceptable gist answers.

I tell the class that none of the previous answers was actually incorrect, but not one of them contained all of what is needed to defend the answer—which makes them not "correct enough." Furthermore, we have only alluded to an answer in each of them; they don't actually reveal a definite answer. Instead, they just throw a few details at us.

Demonstrating Good Self-Based Gists for Our Anchor

For our good gist examples, we'll continue to use the prompts and their restatements from our anchor charts, but we'll extend each restatement onward into the gist answer. Just replicate the sequence of instruction from the restating lesson; that is, before working with the tales and their prompts, use the self-based prompts along with their restatements. The kids need to remain steeped in simplicity, because what lies ahead is a somewhat nebulous phase of the process—one that asks students themselves to develop a gist answer.

We move on by showing students what gist answers sound like; once they hear a few, it's amazing how quickly they catch on and fall in step with the process. So, I demonstrate how the following introductions could be good gist answers—answers that provoke all of the details, but contain none of them.

Restatement with Good Self-Based Gists

Prompt: What do you do in the evening when you get home from school?
Examples of Good Gists:
- In the evening when I get home from school I have fun. *(What do you mean? How do you have fun?)*
- In the evening when I get home from school I sometimes do something unusual and exciting. *(What do you mean? What do you do?)*
- In the evening when I get home from school I enjoy relaxing activities. *(What do you mean? What relaxing activities?)*

What Do You Mean?

After discussing these three samples of good self-based gists, we select one for our self-based anchor, and I hand our green marker to a student so he or she can scribe for us. But before I pull out our other unfinished self-based anchors, I remind the group that we can judge the quality of each gist statement by checking to see if it makes us want to ask, "What do you mean?" That's why, after reading that first answer, *In the evening when I get home from school I have fun*, I turn to the students and ask, "What do you want to ask me?"

In unison they respond, "What do you mean?"

Kiddingly, I answer, "You'll never know, will you? Well, at least not until Step 2, when I provide the details for my gist answer."

Partnering to Debate Acceptable Gists

We move quickly, constructing good gists for each one of the other self-based prompts, and I invite the students into the process along the way. I ask them to chat with their partners and think of a gist statement that relates to each of our self-based anchor restatements, which presently have no gists attached.

After partners have a chance to discuss and maybe debate their good gists, we come back to a whole-class venue so that we can add gists to the other self-based anchor charts. We move through this quickly, and after all this self-based response practice, we're ready to move to the charts that contain our text-based prompts and restatements.

DEVELOPING A TEXT-BASED GIST

After a quick review of gist answers in general, we're ready to investigate some poor text-based ones and some good text-based ones in much the same manner that we did with the self-based—however, this time our gist must be closely related to *text*, not *self*.

Demonstrating Poor Text-Based Gists

I begin by asking students to evaluate a sample set of introductory statements—the top bun for a "Little Red Riding Hood" prompt. We discuss them and decide why each is a poor gist. (This usually takes about two minutes, because by this point, the kids get it!)

Restatements with Poor Text-Based Gists

Prompt: How did the Big Bad Wolf fool Little Red Riding Hood?
Restatements Without Gist Answers:

- The Big Bad Wolf fooled Little Red Riding Hood by going to her grandmother's house and dressing up like Little Red Riding Hood.
- The Big Bad Wolf fooled Little Red Riding Hood by hiding in the grandmother's bed and covering himself up with her blankets.
- The Big Bad Wolf fooled Little Red Riding Hood by putting on her grandmother's nightgown and pulling the covers up.

Demonstrating Good Text-Based Gists

Next, we assess some good introductory statements, making certain we ask after each one: What do you mean?

Restatements with Good Text-Based Gist Answers

- The Big Bad Wolf fooled Little Red Riding Hood by being very clever. *(What do you mean? How was he clever?)*
- The Big Bad Wolf fooled Little Red Riding Hood by anticipating what she would do next. *(What do you mean? What did he anticipate and what did he do about it?)*
- The Big Bad Wolf fooled Little Red Riding Hood by doing something she did not expect. *(What do you mean? What did he do that she did not expect?)*

Each of these gist answers provokes us to investigate more, to ask more questions—which instills the need to back up such statements with facts; that is, every detail that can make our gist statement true or valid. Thus, we come to understand that each of these gists is indeed general enough to serve as an introduction to the rest of the answer. Kids also soon realize that anything remotely close to a gist answer will work, so long as it does not contain details.

Demonstrating a Text-Based Gist for Our Anchor Chart

With all this background under their belts, students are ready to return to the text-based anchors to finish each introduction by adding a gist. Let's start with the "Goldilocks and the Three Bears" anchor. We said, "The three bears were upset when they got home from their walk because . . . " At this point I turn to the kids and say, "Okay, so why were they upset? Let's list the reasons." (Notice that this time I'm working from a collection of details to synthesize a main idea.)

Off the chart, we brainstorm to list the reasons, and afterward I might ask, "Now, these are all the details—but we don't want details right now. So what do all of these things have in common?" It usually doesn't take long before the group starts using words related to the mess the bears found. They may decide on a restatement-gist introduction like the following:

> The three bears were upset when they got home from their walk because their house was not like they left it. *Or one that the kids generally construct:* . . . their house was practically destroyed.

After a couple of these text-based demos, students partner to practice completing the gist for the other text-based restatements (see page 47 for Little Red Riding Hood restatements waiting for a gist to be added). Afterward, as a whole class, we decide on a good gist for each anchor.

After offering students a bit more practice constructing gist answers (see the following activity), we can stretch the concept a bit by introducing the other kind of restatement, a *closed restatement*. We'll investigate the close relationship that exists between gist answers and closed restatements once the students thoroughly understand gist answers.

ACTIVITY

Partnering to Develop Gists

I like to offer the class a bunch of restatements whose gist endings are missing, then invite each of them to select some or all and finish the introduction by adding its gist. Afterward, we share the results.

Prompt: Why did the boy call "Wolf"?
Restatement: The boy called "Wolf" to . . .

Prompt: Why was the beanstalk giant angry with Jack?
Restatement: The beanstalk giant was angry with Jack because . . .

Prompt: Explain how building more bike paths might help the environment.
Restatement: Building more bike paths might help the environment by . . .

Prompt: If you could get your mom anything for Mother's Day (or her birthday), what would you get her? Give reasons for your answer.
Restatement: If I could get my mom anything for Mother's Day, I would get her . . .

ASSESSMENT TYPE: **Test**

At this point it is a good idea to help students understand that these steps should be transferring to their class tests in various subject areas. Therefore, before their assessment, whatever that might be, remind them that their responses to performance prompts should be investigated for restating and gist answers.

FOCUS QUESTIONS

◆ Did you restate using as many words from the questions/petitions as possible?
◆ Did you construct a gist answer for that restatement?
◆ Does your restatement and gist answer make me want to ask, "What do you mean? Explain yourself"?

CLOSED RESTATEMENTS AND GIST ANSWERS: AN INTERESTING MARRIAGE

Once the meaning of a gist answer is steeping, I explain how some prompts lend themselves to a *closed restatement* rather than an open one. In a closed restatement, although the words from the question or petition are restated, that restatement becomes a complete sentence, which ends with a period rather than an ellipsis. Then, I offer the example below, which uses the same prompt to construct an open restatement and a closed one.

Restatements: Open or Closed?

Prompt: Explain how Voldemort tried to fool Harry Potter.
Open Restatement: Voldemort tried to fool Harry Potter by . . .
Closed Restatement #1: Voldemort tried to fool Harry Potter.

The open example ends with an ellipsis, which will be replaced by a gist answer. On the other hand, the closed restatement ends with a period. I often say, "Period!" at the end of a closed restatement, emphasizing what students' ears are telling them. But, open or closed, we need a gist to create the main idea of the paragraph, which neither of these yet possesses. The open restatement needs to be finished with its gist, and the closed restatement needs a stand-alone sentence to offer its gist.

Where Responders Go Wrong Using Closed Restatements

All too often, the period at the end of students' closed restatements fools them into thinking they're ready to move into the body of details or evidence. Yet, they have not introduced those evidential details with their driving force, a main idea. When a closed restatement is devoid of the paragraph's main idea, responders will need a second sentence containing the gist. The following example demonstrates how the previous closed restatement—lacking a gist— has been wedded to a gist sentence:

> *Closed Restatement #2:* Voldemort tried to fool Harry Potter. He did this by using several clever tactics.

Many students fall prey to shallow introductions that, in turn, create shallow evidence and minimal details. That's why I give this the instructional time it needs. In a later chapter, we'll see how multiple-sentence introductions are a necessary feature in multiple-paragraph responses. So this discussion offers a head start into that area.

Next, partner students to use the following examples of closed restatements. Ask them to decide which have the potential to arouse a reader's curiosity and which ones need more gist. Which lead us toward evidence and which appear flat? (And which evoke us to ask, "What do you mean?")

Self-Based Closed Restatements: With or Without a Gist?

- In the evening when I get home from school I enjoy several activities.
- There are many reasons why it is important to be on time for school every day.
- The members of my family enjoy free time together in a number of ways.
- It's important to be on time for school every day.
- People must do lots of things to take proper care of pets.
- Sometimes, I do not know a friend's phone number.

Quantitative Phrasing

Closed restatements that offer a sense of quantification (*several, many, a number of*) generally possess a gist quality about them. This hint at yet-unknown quantities seems to evoke our curiosity, developing a need to know what each of the "several activities" or "many reasons" are. That's why such quantifica-

tion nudges responders toward the details that define or explain each of those several elements. Check the CD for a chart that lists quantitative phrasing.

Closed Restatements Common to Subject-Area Assessments

Quite frequently, content-area assessments contain questions that may be more appropriately answered using a closed restatement. Such questions often call for steps or lists (quantification). Consequently, during the time these subjects are taught, it reinforces the process if we draw attention to any closed restatements evoked by that subject's questions and petitions.

Some closed content-area restatements follow. Sometimes the restatement is closed but incorporates a gist. At other times, we need a follow-up sentence or two to introduce the details. For example, look at these text-based closed restatements from content study:

- The United States was involved in several wars in the twentieth century. Let's see what they had in common.
- The scientific process consists of several steps.
- This mathematical problem can be solved in two ways. However, the second way is faster.
- There is much to be learned from the manner in which the first Americans grew and harvested their food.

Obviously, there would be plenty of alternative wording possibilities for each of these. As long as a student restates the question, it does not matter whether that restatement is open-ended or closed. With that said, I must add that *transitional, open-ended restatements probably slide their creator into the answer more easily*. Ending open restatements with words such as *because* and *by* call forth an answer—a bit like ending a tune on a subdominant note. We can't rest until we hear what comes next.

MORE PRACTICE USING OPEN AND CLOSED RESTATEMENTS

The following examples show how open and closed restatements can be used for the same prompt. It might be interesting to ask students which restatement they think works best in making the writer look better and sound smarter.

Open or Closed? Which Is Better?

Prompt: Why did Little Red Riding Hood think the character in the bed was not her grandmother?
Open: Little Red Riding Hood did not think the character in the bed was her grandmother because . . .
Closed: There are several reasons why Little Red Riding Hood did not think the character in the bed was her grandmother.

Prompt: Why did Jack climb the beanstalk to the giant's castle?
Open: Jack climbed the beanstalk to the giant's castle to . . .
Closed: Let me explain all of the reasons why Jack climbed the beanstalk to the giant's castle.

Prompt: Describe how the three little pigs escaped from the big bad wolf.
Open: The three little pigs escaped from the big bad wolf by . . .
Closed: The three little pigs escaped from the big bad wolf several times by the hair on their chinny-chin chins.

The reason I leave closed restatements until after explaining the gist is because I have found that too many responders circumvent the gist when their restatement ends with a period. If I save it until they understand the gist, I can more easily explain when it has gist qualities and when it doesn't. This can be a tricky piece of the process, so I recommend lots of experience comparing open and closed restatements.

THE KIDS' ABILITIES WILL SURPRISE YOU

Some teachers may anticipate that their students will not be capable of understanding gist. Not so. As a matter of fact, I'll provide a little anecdote as evidence.

After a *Better Answers* workshop, one participant came up to tell me what a child had said to her while she was visiting as a literacy coach in a third-grade classroom—a classroom whose teacher had taught the Better Answer protocol. The coach told me that when she offered a suggestion to a little girl, the child looked up at her and said, "But that's not a gist answer!" That reading specialist was completely taken aback. At that time she had no experience using the protocol, and she found it incredible that this young, identified reading student so completely understood what gist meant. As a matter of fact, the child explained it to the reading teacher. And actually, that is why she ended up in my workshop!

Dramatizing Response for Real-World Interview Questions

With older students, I sometimes liken the Better Answer process to interviewing for a job—a time when everyone wants to look good and sound smart. One way to do this is to restate the interviewer's question, but answer it generally first, and then back up that statement with details. In so doing, the interviewee tends to sound smart. He also sounds organized. Indeed, he sounds like a person a boss would want to hire!

It's fun to dramatize this for students. I play the three roles of interviewer, applicant 1, and applicant 2, bouncing to a different chair each time a character responds. The first applicant uses informal language and body stance, stammers instead of restating, and gets off-topic fast or does not answer the question with any substantial information. The second applicant follows the guidelines of the Better Answer protocol and comes out lookin' good and soundin' smart. Demonstrating this for preteens and teens captures their attention, and I hope will help them perform better in a real interview someday.

IN SEARCH OF GIST TERMS

It's helpful to develop a running list of gist terms so students can begin categorizing what's gist and what's detail. Start them off by offering some examples related to fairy tale characters, settings, or events. For example:
- She was dishonest.
- He was an interesting character.
- The feat was a dangerous one.
- The view was extraordinary!

After each statement, we want to ask, "What do you mean? Explain yourself." A good gist leads responders to elaborate. Students soon come to realize that we will need to explain, describe, or define—to elaborate on—how each term (*dishonest, interesting, dangerous,* and *extraordinary*) is played out in the story in order to support the initial statement.

For a text-based experience, students can focus on characters from a book that has been read in class. Again, we demonstrate before they partner. For instance, referring to *Charlie and the Chocolate Factory,* we might state,
- Charlie is a kind boy. (*What do you mean?*)
- The chocolate factory was a delicious place. (*What do you mean?*)
- Charlie's grandpa was a generous person. (*What do you mean?*)

You can follow the lead I've presented here, but try to weave it into your day. This activity will complement and support your reading curriculum as well as literature response groups (see my book *Knee to Knee, Eye to Eye* [2003]). Simply invite students to work from their own reading materials to develop gist statements (similar to those shown) with a partner.

HASTE MAKES WASTE: REVISITING THE PROMPT

In this day and age of testing, testing, testing, students sometimes take on the traits of robots. They don't think, they just repeat past behaviors. I still smile thinking about a recent experience I had while conferring with some fourth graders. It seemed that some were so anxious to dig in and do the task that they overlooked what the prompt said:

> A new student will be entering your school. Write that student a letter and tell him about some of the most important things he should know about the school . . .

It appeared that several students had jumped right into the task by restating and constructing a gist. The problem was that they forgot that they were supposed to be writing a letter.

Accordingly, I began my one-on-one conferences by asking each to first read the prompt to me. Each of those overzealous responders got as far as the words "Write a letter," at which point every one of them realized his or her error. One read the line twice; another said, "Ohhhh, a letter"; and the third just stopped and looked at me and then at the paper. The look on their faces made me laugh, so each of them laughed too. It's easy to make silly mistakes when we are acting robotically rather than thinking.

Surely, we want the kids to feel confident. And we want them to move into the task with interest. But we do not want to create robots. So before responders put the pen to the paper, they will always want to carefully consider the form their writing will take, because a letter is not an email is not a poem is not a story is not a . . .

Classroom Vignette

Demonstrating Step 1: Develop an Introduction

Before we move on into Step 2, let's "watch" the first step in process through a vignette set in a grade 5 classroom. Notice how the teacher demonstrates, yet opens the process to invite students in.

Ms. Diaz finishes reading "The Boy Who Cried Wolf," and after placing the book on her desk, she lifts the top page of a large classroom chart to reveal a prompt:

Why did the boy continue to cry wolf when there was no wolf?

The prompt is written on a sentence strip, but temporarily adhered to a piece of chart paper, the space underneath inviting an answer.

"Our first prompt's an easy one—just one sentence, and it's a question. No background information. No petitions. So who wants to be our restatement marker as we work with the first prompt? You'll need to underline and substitute words as the restating helper restates," the teacher explains. Juan looks interested, so Ms. Diaz responds, "Juan, want to be our marker for this first question?"

"Okay," Juan answers as he moves to the chart and picks up the black marker resting on the ledge of the chalkboard. At this point Ms. Diaz removes the strip from the chart and tapes it to the front board so that both marker and responder have room to do their jobs.

As she does this, she extends a second invitation to the group. "Okay, who will volunteer to be our scribe for writing out the dictations given during Step 1 of the Better Answer protocol? Cindi, would you like to do it, since you did not have a chance yet?"

"I hope you can read my writing," Cindi responds as she walks to the blank chart paper. Glancing back at the class questioningly, Cindi reaches for a green marker sitting in a cup on her teacher's desk.

"It'll be fine, Cindi. Remember that this is just a rough, working draft. I'm sure we'll be able to read it," supports her teacher. However, she then adds, "But do remember to use the prompt as a spelling reference to copy correctly for the restatement part, please. These words are ones everyone should spell correctly because they are right there for us." Ms. Diaz then points to the sentence and begins.

"So, the first prompt is 'Why did the boy continue to cry wolf when there was no wolf?' Let's restate first. Louie, would you please restate that for us?" the teacher requests, certain that Louie will competently handle her invitation.

Louie responds, "Well, uh, uh, let's see—The boy continued to . . . " and as Louie moves on with the restatement, Juan underlines and marks the original sentence in the following manner:

continued
Why did <u>the</u> <u>boy</u> ~~continue~~ <u>to</u> <u>cry</u> <u>wolf</u> <u>when</u> <u>there</u> <u>was</u> <u>no</u> <u>wolf</u>?

Louie continues, " . . . cry wolf when there was no wolf because—" He stops just after saying "because" and before he becomes involved in the answer.

At this point, Ms. Diaz steps forward. "Thanks, Louie! You stopped just in the right place." Juan, the marker, goes back to his seat as Ms. Diaz turns to Cindi, who is writing Louie's restatement on the chart.

As Cindi is completing the last word, Ms. Diaz compliments, "Hey, Cindi, that's a great job of scribing you did for us! Go ahead and reread it to make sure all is well, and we'll move on to the gist answer.

"Now, let's think of a gist answer to the question, Why did the boy keep crying wolf? Remember: No specifics! No details! Just a general, gist answer—one that will make us want to ask, 'What do you mean?'" Ms. Diaz prompts.

Tamar, always eager to speak up, offers, "I think it should be something about him looking for attention, or maybe trying to show off."

The teacher remains quiet, waiting for someone to respond to either Tamar or to the question. After a somewhat long, silent void the teacher suggests, "All right, let's try to work off Tamar's suggestion—unless someone else has a suggestion?"

When no one responds she says, "Do you think the boy was looking for attention? Was he showing off? Joe, what do you think?"

"I think he was trying to get everyone all excited because he was bored," Joe suggests.

"So, that is similar to what Tamar is saying. How would you finish the restatement then? What would your gist answer be? What should Cindi write?" The teacher restates the part that has already been written: "The boy continued to cry wolf when there was no wolf because . . . " and she smiles, raising her eyebrows at Joe to encourage his response.

Joe follows her lead with "Because . . . because he wanted to get everyone excited because he was bored."

"Okay, let's go for it!" the teacher says as she turns to Cindi again and adds, "Let's give Cindi a hand with the spelling because now she has no cues from the question." But, Cindi has confidently completed half the sentence before the teacher and the class begin their spelling support. In the end, Joe's gist answer finishes the first sentence on the chart.

Afterward the teacher asks, "What do you think, friends? Here is what we have so far: 'The boy continued to cry wolf when there was no wolf because he wanted to get everyone excited because he was bored.'"

"I think there are too many becauses," interjects Ilia.

"Well, how could we fix that? How could we make it sound better?" Ms. Diaz asks.

"Could we say, 'The boy continued to cry wolf when there was no wolf because he was bored and wanted to get everyone excited?'" offers Cindi, taking the lead at the front of the room.

"What do you think now, friends?" the teacher inquires. The group nods, affirming Cindi's revision.

So, Cindi dictates her own revised ending while at the same time writing it. "Looks like a one-woman band!" the teacher adds jokingly. Cindi seems pleased.

"Okay, so now let's read what Cindi has written for us, and then we can move on to restating and answering a second prompt." Ms. Diaz sticks the prompt strip back on the chart and continues, "Later, I'd like you to work with your partner to create some prompts of your own. Choose a fairy tale or fable we've read. Remember, you can use the Question Menu, and don't forget to include some petitions too.

"Afterward, you can exchange papers with another pair of partners. Then, they can use Step 1 to respond to your prompts, and you can do the same for theirs.

"Remember, though," the teacher adds, "we'll soon be moving on to Step 2, the supporting details, so after you finish your practice with your partner, I think I will keep your papers, and we can use them again when we get to the next two steps—when we'll be able to add details that'll support your answers and a concluding statement. Eventually, you will be doing this independently, just as you'll have to do on a test—or even in a job interview. But, for now, let's work with partners."

INCORPORATING WHAT WE'VE LEARNED SO FAR

The further we venture into the protocol, the easier it is to see how it connects to all subjects. As a matter of fact, by the time all of the steps are completed, the protocol should have become enveloped in the ongoing curriculum. That means that it will be continually reinforced and reviewed, eventually becoming second nature to the students.

By this point, it proves beneficial to encourage the use of Step 1 during any performance assessment done in class. The fact that students have not been taught all the steps does not preclude the implementation of those they do understand. As a matter of fact, I'm always surprised just how fast they do pick up on this first part of the process. And, the faster they internalize Step 1, the sooner they'll be ready to understand the importance of Step 2.

CHAPTER 5

STEP

2

BUILD A BODY
OF DETAILS

Concreteness is now seen as necessary and unavoidable only as a stepping stone for developing abstract thinking—as a means, not an end in itself.
—Lev Vygotsky, *Mind and Society*

In preparation for teaching Step 2, I again reach for the Better Answer Sandwich chart. During our quick review, I draw attention to the sandwich's middle layers while reminding the students how each of the sections work together to create a whole and cohesive paragraph. Afterward, I again post the Sandwich chart in a conspicuous and permanent spot.

Writing: II.5, II.6, II.7

STEP 2: BUILD A BODY OF DETAILS

Now that the gist answer is constructed, it should point the responder directly toward the details that will back the gist, and thus, Step 2 unfolds quite naturally out of Step 1. For a self-based response, the body of details is evoked through personal reflection and followed by note taking. But in text-based responses, we construct the sandwich middle by returning to the text to search for as many details as we can find; these text details should provide evidence we need to support the introduction's gist or thesis statement. But whether writing a text-based or self-based response, we are led by that begging question, "What do you mean?"

Every responder who understands how to construct a restatement and a gist answer has had little trouble locating supporting details, because completing the first step narrows the search. Yet, finding the details is only one part of Step 2; students must also decide the order of presentation, plan how to incorporate those details into sentences that will make a coherent and cohesive paragraph, and do all this in an interesting style.

The best way to accomplish all this is through teacher demonstration, ongoing writing experiences, and individual scaffolding based on mindful assessment practices, which involve reading a variety of responses. A considerable task! But the Better Answer protocol will help you and your students succeed.

THE KEY TEACHING STRATEGY: TEACHER THINK-ALOUDS

Each time we humans hope to learn a process—be it swimming, dancing, response-writing, or stargazing—we first want to see it done. Learners initially mimic models before they can perform a task independently. Therefore, just showing students a variety of written responses is not enough, because it does not reveal the ways in which we writers think through the writing task. Showing finished products provides important background knowledge, but we need to expose the sometimes messy process of how finished products unfold into their final form.

During any writing task, the voice in our heads helps us clarify, connect, create, and compose ideas. Have you ever chatted to yourself when you've misplaced your keys? We all do that, because talk helps us solve problems. That same covert voice chatters to us during writing, too, but we must bring it to the surface so students can hear how we think.

Think-Alouds and Write-Alouds (TAWAs)

Think-alouds and write-alouds (TAWAs) interpret covert thinking into overt processes that occur during spontaneous writing. Through TAWAs, students are able to observe the myriad thoughts that evoke the writing process.

My first TAWA demonstrations help the students to feel more comfortable. Yet, because these demos are spontaneous, they can be a bit intimidating for the teacher because she or he cannot plan exact moves. After the first few TAWAs, though, they are actually fun and end up weaving their way into many periods of my teaching. Furthermore, the kids love them because they can observe their instructor in a state of semi-confusion—a time when their teacher does not know all the answers. After all, even adults request, "Don't just tell me, show me." Certainly, TAWAs are important for many reasons.

When we teachers share our own mind's journey as it searches for details and then synthesizes them into a connected piece of writing, our students come to understand what's inside the process. The TAWA is therefore an essential, strategic technique. (The classroom vignette at the end of Chapter 6 demonstrates a TAWA lesson.)

A TAWA FOR A SELF-BASED RESPONSE

Let's consider what a think-aloud might include if we use it with that first self-based prompt from Step 1:

What do you do in the evening when you get home from school?

We completed Step 1 for this prompt by restating and constructing a gist answer:

In the evening when I get home from school, I do some work, but also save time to play.

For a Step 2 think-aloud, a teacher would reread the sentence and then share aloud the next steps her mind takes. She may say, "What do I mean by 'I do some work'? What kind of work and what kind of play? Hmm, I guess I could first list all the work and play activities."

Implementing the TAWA

Entering the process in this manner leads right into drafting some detail-related notes by jotting down various "pieces" of play and work. As they arise in my mind, I say them aloud as I write them, but not necessarily in a particular order. I tell the kids that I can order those pieces and develop each into sound sentences *after* I have my comprehensive list.

So, I stumble aloud along my brain's path leading to a number of "work and play" possibilities, only some of which I keep and write down, while others get tossed. Regardless, I continue to reveal what my brain is reasoning: what work and play means to me in the evenings. Once I'm pleased with my details search, I discuss the next hurdle: the order in which I will present those details.

ORDERING DETAILS

We can order details in a number of ways. The following are the most common:

Ways to Order Details
- chronological order: the way in which things happen along a time line
- order of importance: revealing details from most important to least important or vice versa
- order of prompt: for prompts that have several parts, we answer in the order in which questions and/or petitions are presented in the prompt

I think the last order, the order of the prompt, is the most important to teach. Not only is it important during performance assessment, but it's just as valuable when our employer issues a prompt with several petitions or questions in it. In both cases we want the reader of our response to know that we respect the prompt's organization and that we have indeed included all of its requested parts. Therefore, it makes good sense to stick to the order that was indicated in the prompt. If we change that order, it may appear to a busy boss or a distracted test corrector that the responder forgot to include something. So why not just give those readers the order they expect?

USING TRANSITIONS AS GLUE

When used appropriately, transitions, such as *first*, *next*, or *however*, can make a writer look good and sound smart. There are actually a wide variety of these terms, which can be used as connectors and help glue the sentences of a paragraph together. Through lots of use, these handy terms eventually become internalized, but I always demonstrate their use during think-alouds and even more so during individual writing conferences.

The Transitions Sandwich (see Figure 5 and the CD) offers a ready reference menu. (Restatement Transitions and Transitions for Every Purpose also can be found on the CD.) Note that there are no hard and fast rules related to sequential usage of these. For example, the term *finally* might be used toward the end of the layered details, rather than in the concluding statement. And you'll notice in Figure 5, the Transitions Sandwich, that most introductions and conclusions incorporate phrases, rather than single-word transitions as the body of details does. Nevertheless, this ordered chart is a handy reference tool for all responders.

Figure 5

Transitions Sandwich

Use Transitions to Sound Smart!

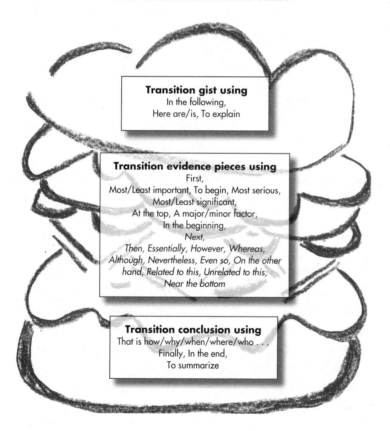

Transition gist using
In the following,
Here are/is, To explain

Transition evidence pieces using
First,
Most/Least important, To begin, Most serious,
Most/Least significant,
At the top, A major/minor factor,
In the beginning,
Next,
Then, Essentially, However, Whereas,
Although, Nevertheless, Even so, On the other
hand, Related to this, Unrelated to this,
Near the bottom

Transition conclusion using
That is how/why/when/where/who . . .
Finally, In the end,
To summarize

DEMONSTRATING STEP 2 FOR OUR SELF-BASED ANCHOR

It makes sense for my evening activities response to be in chronological order, the way the activities usually happen after I get home, so I explain that decision to the group. Then, as I am numbering each detail in my brainstormed list, I think aloud why I am doing it in that manner. For example, "First, I go for a walk, so that's 1 and it's play. Then, after making supper, I do the dishes, so that's 2—dishes are work, but sometimes cooking is play." This is only the first half of the detailing step, because once our notes are numbered, we have to get those details together in a connected text, a paragraph body.

Using a TAWA to Connect the Pieces into a Cohesive Whole

I grab my blue marker, the color I use for Step 2, and the unfinished anchor chart and say, "Let's see. How shall I start?" as I begin to compose. Then, I reread the restatement and the attached gist answer: "In the evening when I get home from school, I do some work, but also save time to play." I think aloud as I start to compose the body of details in sentence format. "I'll start with number 1 first. This one: 'go for walk.' How will I say that? I know, I'll say, 'If it's a nice day I always go for a walk with my dog, Jesse.' I'm elaborating a bit about the nice day and dog to make it more interesting—more details. Some elaboration makes writing more interesting, but I'll be careful that I don't get off-topic," I explain. So I scribe this new sentence right after the gist answer, which means that I have now offered one detail to back up the fact that I had fun:

> In the evening when I get home from school, I do some work but also save time to play. *If it's a nice day I always go for a walk with my dog, Jesse.*

At this point I might turn to the class and ask, "How am I doing?" Of course, they usually think the teacher is doing fine—at first.

I continue in this manner, debating various elements along the way, for example, whether I should describe any experiences that happen during my walks. I decide to tell a little bit about the walk, because what happens along the way is what makes it fun—play. It backs up my gist. "I must describe those experiences that were play," I say, "experiences that provide evidence for my gist." I keep reviewing this strategy in this manner. (You will read more about this strategy in the vignette at the end of Chapter 6.)

When the paragraph body feels finished, I reread all that I've written and talk my way through any edits I deem necessary. In the end, it might look something like this (note that I purposely try *not* to be too fanciful. After all, we don't want to intimidate the kids with more advanced writing during initial lessons):

> In the evening when I get home from school, I do some work, but also save time to play. First of all, if it's a nice day, I always go for a walk

with my dog, Jesse. We have fun with our dog friends and people friends on the beach. Afterward, I get busy making something interesting for supper, for example, pesto pasta or quinoa salad. Sometimes, I invite friends to join me. Once the meal is over, the kitchen is clean, and the dishes are done, I figure I deserve some downtime. So I check my email and watch the news. I may do another chore, too, but eventually, I pick up a book I've started and enjoy reading before I finally roll back the covers and jump into bed.

To emphasize the necessity of rereading, I reread one more time and finally ask, "How's it sound? Any tweaks?"

Partnering into Independent Self-Based Responses

After my modeling, I grab another of the self-based anchors we used in Step 1. Together the class and I work through the steps composing together. Afterward, I invite the students to try their hand at a sandwich middle. I display a couple more of our earlier self-based anchors, encourage them to select one, and after copying its introduction onto their own paper, move on to compose their own details.

"Once you decide what you plan to do, discuss it with a partner. Explain some of the details you'll use, then once you get those details numbered, share again to see what your partner thinks." Talking is excellent rehearsal for writing.

After students finish the detailed bodies of their paragraphs, I ask some to read theirs to us. We then draw straws to see whose will be copied onto our ongoing anchor charts.

DEMONSTRATING STEP 2 FOR TEXT-BASED RESPONSE ANCHORS

Now let's investigate a text-based body of details. If we use a read-aloud, students will not usually have a text in front of them to locate the details. In instances where they do, however, they may use underlining or highlighting, or certainly those handy sticky notes, to mark important details. Obviously, note taking while the teacher reads the text aloud is always a possibility too.

You might prefer to use demonstration transparencies and project the text using an overhead, because it will allow you to mark up the text during a common viewing/reading experience. In the end, it's probably a good idea to demonstrate different options, but note taking while the teacher reads aloud remains the most versatile.

The Answer Organizer

At this point in the process, most teachers find that the Answer Organizer (Figure 6) is a handy tool, because it directly channels students along the path we want them to follow. On a double-entry page, the Answer Organizer shows the sandwich's three parts listed in the left column and leaves space to write in the right column. And don't forget the color belonging to each part.

Figure 6

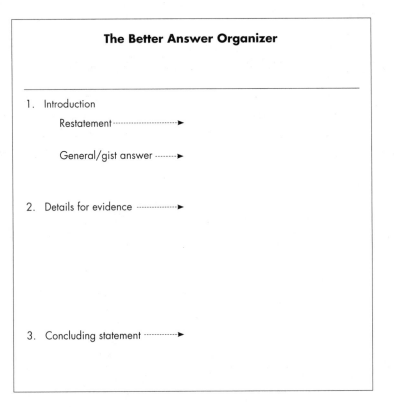

The Better Answer Organizer

1. Introduction
    Restatement ----------------➤

    General/gist answer --------➤

2. Details for evidence -------------➤

3. Concluding statement -----------➤

Other Charts and Visuals

    Also, the Petition Framework (Figure 2 on page 27 and on the CD) can be especially helpful when developing this body of details, because it too aids the organization process. So this is a good time to pull it out again.

Using the Petition Framework to Develop a Body of Details

I've already quite thoroughly discussed the Petition Framework, but as we develop this body of details, I feel the need to point out its relevance again. The chart offers a possible direction for developing a body of details for many common petitions. For example, let's say the term *explain* or *explain why* is used in the prompt. The Petition Framework indicates that when that term is used, it is helpful for writers to develop a T-chart, placing major facts in the left column with supportive details in the right. Thus, it is an organizational tool, and organizing a piece of writing is sometimes the toughest part. So when asked to explain, a T-chart can help.

I'd pull that Petition Framework chart out of your coffers and keep it handy as you move through multiple prompts and their responses. Enlarge and post it on a wall. That way, it's there to help writers organize their writing anytime they get stuck.

Partnering Through the Details

Figure 7, a "Little Red Riding Hood" prompt and response, shows sections of the Answer Organizer (this figure is also on the CD) that have already been completed. This can serve as a model and instructional support. I use it as a guide for a lesson to demonstrate a text-based reading response, but I cover up the conclusion so students don't see it until Step 3 in the process. After I've demonstrated the process, I leave it as a developing anchor.

Figure 7

The Better Answer Organizer

Question: How did Little Red Riding Hood know that the character in the bed was not her grandmother?

1. Introduction

   Restatement ------------➤ *Little Red Riding Hood knew that the character in the bed was not her grandmother*

   General/gist answer ------------➤ *because that character did not look or sound like her grandmother.*

2. Details for evidence ------------➤ *She noticed that his voice was gruff, not like her grandmother's voice. Also, that character in the bed had very large eyes, unlike her grandmother's. But most important, what she noticed were his teeth. They were huge!*

3. Concluding statement ------------➤ *That is how Little Red Riding Hood knew that character was not her grandmother, and it's a good thing she noticed!*

After I've demonstrated how to construct a body of details for this text-based prompt, I suggest that partners mimic what I've demonstrated. With the Answer Organizer for "Goldilocks and the Three Bears" (see Figure 8) in mind—but not in sight—I read its correlated tale and introduce the prompt and the introduction. I don't show them my completed organizer yet. Instead, I ask partners to copy the already-composed introduction onto a blank Answer Organizer, and then together develop the body of details. I remind them to use the organizer's visual sequence, but jot their list of details onto a piece of scrap paper so they can organize and sequence them before composing the body.

I observe and scaffold as they wade into the process, and after they've had time to develop some details, I interrupt to invite the partners to offer possibilities. I scribe their ideas onto a large chart in no particular order. Afterward, we organize the scribed notes for everyone to use.

To organize the scribed notes, we first decide what order will make sense to best support our gist answer. Next, we select the place each detail will hold, numbering them 1, 2, 3, and so on. Some we decide not to use. Consequently, the list gets pared to only the most essential details, as we continually ask, "Do I really need this to support the gist answer?"

After we have numbered the details, I ask partners to compose each into a sentence, just as I did before. At this time I strongly encourage the use of transitions to connect sentence pieces into a cohesive whole. Transitions offer such obvious glue to a piece that each becomes a small anchor for lookin' good and soundin' smart.

Later, dyads have a chance to read aloud what they've constructed. Each will differ, but each should follow a very similar path. This kind of gradual release of ownership develops writing confidence so that as students move into independent realms, they feel more secure. When all is said and done, I display my completed "Goldilocks and the Three Bears" Answer Organizer (with its conclusion masked) and ask partners to compare it with their paragraphs, always assuring them that the basic facts may be the same, but that there are many ways to put those facts into a cohesive whole.

Work done collaboratively irons out the wrinkles while developing confidence in the process. With whole-class scaffolding and partners continually rereading and discussing their writing, the entire process is sure to make more sense. Partners learn that when they change their minds—when they must come to a common decision and cross things out to revise—the end product is far better. Yes, writing is a messy process.

Throughout that week, I continue to give opportunities for partners and then individuals to develop details for our other text-based anchor charts. But I also focus on integrating that learning into the entire curriculum.

After these experiences, we're ready to develop an ending for our pieces. But before we move on to Step 3 and the bottom bun, there are a couple of items I want to address. First, I introduce a handy checklist, and later, a few more ideas and activities related to Step 2.

Figure 8

The Better Answer Organizer

Question: Why were the three bears so upset when they got home from their walk?

---

1. Introduction

    Restatement ----------------> *The three bears were upset when they got home because*

    General/gist answer --------> *their house was not like they left it.*

2. Details for evidence -------> *To begin with, the bears noticed that someone had been eating their porridge. Next they discovered that someone had broken Baby Bear's chair. Furthermore, their beds were messed up. Most important, however, was that there was a little girl IN one of the beds!*

3. Concluding statement -------> *As a result of all that confusion the three bears were very upset.*

ASSESSING ◆ CONFERRING

ASSESSMENT TYPE: Topic Checklist

During this step I present a rather simple checklist to help students evaluate the veracity of their details. This checklist asks only three questions, but students must sign off on each before sharing work with me or anyone else.

Sometimes I have them partner, read their complete answers to each other, and then discuss the answer to each of these questions together.

FOCUS QUESTIONS

- ◆ Did I prove my answer?
- ◆ Does what I wrote make sense? (And, did I reread to see if it does?)
- ◆ What would a stranger ask me about what I wrote?

EXACT FACTS OR COOL AND CREATIVE FICTION?

Novices can confuse text-based and self-based writing, which becomes evident when they move into independent response. I find that at least one student will slide into creative writing in the midst of a test response; that is, Manuel may compose a beautiful constructed response and, just as he is trying to conclude the piece, he might slip into fantasy and concoct a completely new ending for the text he read. Instead of saying a character should've, would've, or could've, he says the character actually did it! Not "Goldilocks should never go back into that house again," but rather, "Goldilocks never went back into that house again." The former may be a somewhat clever ending; the latter is just plain inappropriate. But can you feel the fine line that exists between the two for a young child?

I observed as fourth grader Sean meandered off the story line during a lesson. I had read the fable of the "Bear and the Bees" to the group, and he had responded to the prompt's question quite nicely, adhering to specific details from the story. But then, at the very end of his little essay response, he deviated. Instead of saying what Bear *could* have done or what *might* happen the next time Bear encountered a similar situation, he began telling what Bear did next—when there was no next! Instead of constructing a conclusion, Sean threw the facts away and constructed a whole new ending to the story.

Other students take similar wrong turns in their responses, especially when their teacher advises, "Add more voice." They add small fabrications here and there because they think it is clever or makes their writing more interesting. Just today Maria told us that the bear "grabbed the log with his teeth, showed his claws, and growled." The bear did the first two things, but Maria was on a roll, so she just extended it a bit with a small embellishment. To a child's way of thinking, this makes the response even better, but I explain to them that it is not appropriate for this kind of task. Nor is it appropriate for many real-world tasks.

The fine lines existing in these situations make clarifying difficult. Consistent use of the Boundaries Scale helps, but I found another tool to use too. First, I explain how some adult tasks require us to be "cool and creative," and other tasks call for us to present the "exact facts." For example, a landscaper who runs into a problem may need a worker who has some cool and creative ideas she could commit to print, but a newspaper reporter stationed in a war zone would be expected to report only the facts. When presented this way, most kids understand the lines of demarcation here. But it helps to suggest that they act much like news reporters when they are taking a performance assessment. That is, they should not be cool and creative *unless* the task does indeed ask them to write creatively. Otherwise, they should act like a reporter and stick to exact facts. Certainly, reading exemplars will help direct their efforts. And so will the following activity.

Fact or Fiction?

So that students may more fully understand what is appropriate to include in a response, I construct a T-chart. I label the left side "Exact Facts" and the right side "Cool and Creative," and begin the lesson by reading aloud a short story or tale such as "Goldilocks and the Three Bears." When I finish, I give each student a copy of the story. I also pass out index cards on some of which I have written a story-related fact, whereas others contain a fictional sentence or phrase.

Each student then takes a turn to come and place his or her card under the heading best suited for it. But, as the student does this, he or she knows to be prepared to answer the question: Why do you think your card belongs in that column? Some examples follow.

For instance, if we use "Goldilocks and the Three Bears" (the version on the CD, whose wording is cited in parentheses), some facts may be the following:

- Goldilocks's mother was often afraid. ("a fearful sort")
- Goldilocks could tell Mama Bear's porridge was hot, so she passed it up. ("noticed steam rising . . . thus circumvented it")
- Papa Bear comforted his daughter when she was upset. ("to console her . . . picked her up . . . hugged her")

Fairy Tales and Fables

Although these statements are facts from the story, I did not state them in exactly the same manner that the story did. They are sound inferences based on facts. For that reason, to prove their point students need to return to the story's evidence for their choice of card placement.

It's easy to see how kids might confuse reworded, inferential statements with creative deviations from the facts. It also demonstrates why *inferential thinking* is a comprehension strategy (Harvey and Goudvis 2007).

The following examples could be placed in the "cool and creative" column:

- The police are going to arrest Goldilocks for breaking and entering.
- Goldilocks's mother does not care about her, or she would not allow her child to roam the woods alone.
- The bears spent a lot of time cleaning up after Goldilocks.

This last example is a very common type of error, because it is actually a post-story prediction. Students who have been appropriately encouraged to predict "what happens next" throughout primary-grade reading lessons sometimes use that path when it is inappropriate. So it's worth drawing attention to the difference between textual information and that which our own imaginations create.

Lastly, although very careful consideration should be given to discouraging use of cool and creative statements on many performance assessments, it's a good idea to ask students to decide what might be an occasion when those cool and creative responses *would be* appropriate. We do want students to be cool and creative; we just don't want them to misuse such writing on exact-fact tests.

INVITE "THE STRANGER" IN

As writers crawl into the details of a piece, they often forget their audience, and they write as though the reader already possesses background information. At this point I invite "the Stranger" into the classroom. This technique was developed out of an immediate need when I was conferring with students in Barb McKay's fourth-grade class. Barb had been working with the Better Answer protocol and had asked me, as the school's literacy coach, to come in and help "grease the wheels" where it was needed.

I decided to start with individual conferences, the most effective technique for scaffolding students. During those conferences, I noticed a kind of pattern among the group—a pattern I had seen the previous year when working with fifth-grade students. That is, they tended to write as if the reader would already know much of the information—information that they consequently omitted.

Such lack of awareness of audience causes students to overdose on pronouns (*She left her when her mother . . .*), use lone referents (*They didn't go there because of what happened*), and omit important evidence that could support their answers. Unfortunately, this minimalist approach leaves the reader of such a response clueless. This neglect to consider an audience was exactly what I was observing in those fourth-grade responses, and I struggled to bring this problem into the students' awareness.

Gropingly, I asked one fourth-grader with whom I was working, "Sonya, what if the principal, or some stranger, came down the hall and read this? Think about it. What would that stranger want to know if he read only your answer?" I then got up, walked down the hall a few feet, and returned personifying "the Stranger."

"Oh, hi, little girl. I'm from Channel 4 and we are visiting your school today to see what the students are doing," I pretended. "What's this you're doing? Is it okay if I read over your shoulder?"

"Sure," laughed Sonya, playing along.

So I began to read over her shoulder, "In the story 'The Lion and the Mouse' the mouse proved the lion was wrong because he—Hmm, he? He? Does Sonya mean the mouse?" I muttered loudly enough so Sonya could hear my covert thinking. "Or he, the lion? . . . because he got him out from being caught. Hmm, who got whom out? And what was he caught in? What does she mean?"

After my Stranger act, Sonya responded, "Oh, I get it. I have to explain it more!"

"Exactly. And replace all those pronouns with nouns, because the Channel 4 anchorwoman does not know who the hes and shes are," I suggested. "Just keep thinking that the Stranger is standing over your shoulder observing your response. What would she want to know? What would bother her and make her go, 'Huh? What does she mean?'"

Later, I shared with Sonya's teacher what I had done with Sonya, as well as several others who also needed the Stranger looking over their shoulders. Barb, their teacher, thought it sounded like a good idea and said she would continue to use it. We also discussed how it would be helpful if, the next time her class answered some questions, the other fourth-grade group could read them and act as the Strangers.

A couple of weeks later Barb stopped me in the hall and exclaimed, "The Stranger is working wonders in our room! I wish he had visited in September!"

We also came to realize that if the Stranger is unable, simply by reading the answer, to infer the question that was being asked, then the answer is not complete. In other words, every answer should be able to stand alone and make sense without its question. It should be a small stand-alone essay. This is important for students to understand.

Since that time I have shared the Stranger with many other teachers and kids and have taken him or her to a variety of other classrooms from grades 3 through 8. That Stranger works wonders every time! The teachers and I have even put on coats and hats and disguised our voices to add more realism. In School 45 in Buffalo, the curriculum director, Mary Ann Hopfer, asked the art teacher to make "Stranger" posters with a few writers' guidelines for all classrooms in grades 3 through 8! They now hang as ready reminders to write for an audience, one of whom might be the Stranger.

I only wish the Stranger had visited the reading classes I taught at the university, because my college students often displayed some of the same shortcomings in their writing. Even in reviewing journal articles for two professional organizations, I continually write in the margins, asking the author the same questions that the Stranger would ask. Obviously, the Stranger is going to have a very big job ahead of her, so it's best to invite her in ASAP!

TIME TO REVISIT THE PROMPT CHAPTER

The strategies related to prompts (discussed in Chapter 2) wind right into the development of the introduction and the body. It's the natural way that prewriting unfolds into writing.

So at this point in the developing paragraph sandwich, it's a good idea to revisit the strategies for understanding the prompt from this book's second chapter. I like to review thick and thin prompts/responses, the Boundaries Scale, the Petition Framework, the Question Menu, and any other items that seem relevant to the particular group of students I am teaching.

I exit Step 2 by asking: "Are we looking good and sounding smart yet?"

By this point the entire class usually cheers a confident, "Yes!"

COMING UP: THAT FINAL STEP

Just as prewriting unfolds into writing, the introduction and the body unfold into a concluding statement. Yet once responders finish the body, many feel that they have already produced a correct answer—and indeed they may have. However, their paragraph *will not sound smart unless it sounds finished* (Ardie Cole's mantra). For a better answer, each response needs a concluding statement. Let's move on and see how easily this final step unfolds.

CHAPTER 6

STEP

3

DRAW A
CONCLUSION

Go on till you come to the end: then stop.
—Lewis Carroll, *Alice's Adventures in Wonderland*

Hooray! The end is near. But before I introduce Step 3 in the Better Answer Protocol, I again reach for the Answer Sandwich chart to review the steps I've modeled and the students have experienced. After our review, it's time to introduce the bottom bun. I begin with music.

Why would I teach conclusions using music? I want students to understand that, unless we signal listeners or readers that a piece is finished, they may be left hanging. To demonstrate why both music and writing need to sound finished, I sing the musical scale, but stop before the final C. "Makes you want to finish it, doesn't it?" I ask. "Well, that's how readers feel when you don't add an ending to a piece of writing."

Writing: II.8, II.9

Of course you don't have to sing if you don't want to. You could use a CD recording, stopping it on a subdominant note. Or you could read a short story and stop before the end. Bottom line: These analogies work.

RESTATE THE RESTATEMENT

Authors of writers' guides frequently suggest an easy way to end a response, report, or essay—use a *circular closing*. In a circular closing, the ending repeats a phrase or part that was prominent in the beginning. In the case of a response, the writer would repeat the restatement (part of the top bun).

For struggling students or those in a hurry, simply restating the restatement (from Step 1) is one of the easiest—and most used—methods of ending a piece. We merely begin with the words "That is how . . . " or "That is why . . . " and mimic the restatement. For example, we might say: "That is why the three bears were so upset when they got home." Even columnists and well-known writers sometimes end a paragraph in this manner.

Essentially, that final restatement asserts that we have done what we said we would do in the introduction. But it also makes the piece sound finished—and the writer sound smart.

USE TERMINAL TERMS AND FINAL PHRASING

There are specific transitions that signal the end is near—words like *finally, lastly, in closing,* and *in conclusion*. Check the Transitions Sandwich on the CD and on page 69. Adding one of these to the concluding statement offers its readers that sense of finality that is usually evident in a successful response. Invite students to play with various terminal terms so that they have a feel for which may suit a given purpose.

Better Answer
Transitions Charts

A TOUCH OF VOICE: MAKING CONNECTIONS

Once students gain the confidence and competence to construct an introduction and a body of details, I scaffold them toward incorporating a touch of voice into this concluding section. One of the easiest techniques involves a comprehension strategy called "making connections" (Harvey and Goudvis 2007). I suggest students make the following types of connections in that bottom bun:

- a personal connection
- a world connection
- a text connection
- a craft connection

I believe it's important to save these connections for the very end of a Better Answer response or an employee's report—*after* all questions and petitions have been addressed. That is not to say, however, that on *all* essays voice should be squeezed into those final lines. There are multiple essay types where voice is indeed woven in and out and about, for instance, those we hear daily on National Public Radio, in Amazon.com book reviews, and in responses to narrative writing prompts. However, when we encourage young students to try to weave voice into the middle of their constructed responses on tests, they often get carried away and go off on a tangent. Saving personal reflections, opinions, and connections for the end leaves the reader with a taste of voice, yet limits the writer on the amount. It also keeps the student from tainting the body of details, which have already been presented.

A whole book could be written related to the kinds of connections that can be made in a conclusion. It's not always easy to teach these connections to students, so I suggest lots of think-alouds. Harvey and Goudvis (2007) provide wonderful background for instructional strategies related to this connections process.

A Touch of Voice: Adding Humor

This concluding statement is also the part of a response where a touch of humor can be woven in. Offering several examples and inviting ideas from the students seems to open the door to humor (even if things do get a bit silly at times). I find kids easily catch on to how tongue-in-cheek can be woven in. Furthermore, they enjoy it! I tell them that we want to leave the reader smiling—be it a test corrector or our boss.

CONCLUDING OUR SELF-BASED PROMPT

After I have my evolving self-based prompt in hand, I grab a red marker (the color for *stop*), and we're ready to focus on finishing. I begin by rereading the prompt as well as what I've written so far.

> *Prompt:* What do you do in the evening when you get home from school?
>
> *Response:* In the evening when I get home from school, I do some work, but also save time to play. First of all, if it's a nice day, I always go for a walk with my dog, Jesse. We have fun with our dog friends and people friends on the beach. Afterward, I get busy making something interesting for supper, for example, pesto pasta or quinoa salad. Sometimes, I invite friends to join me. Once the meal is over, the kitchen is clean, and

the dishes are done, I figure I deserve some downtime. So I check my email and watch the news. I may do another chore, too, but eventually, I pick up a book I've started and enjoy reading before I finally roll back the covers and jump into bed.

After reading the unfinished response, we have fun playing with a variety of concluding statements. In my think-alouds, at first I lean heavily on terminal terms and circular conclusions, and usually settle on a conclusion that incorporates one of them. So we might use this one:

That's often what I do in the evening when I get home from school.

Yet, I indicate that I'm not quite satisfied because I'd like to leave my reader with a smile on his or her face. I want something just a tad clever. So what could I say that would do that? After pondering a few ideas, I settle on the following concluding statement:

That's often what I do in the evening when I get home from school. I bet you do some of those same things too.

Concluding statements are easy—and fun, if you invite the kids to work together in small groups. Divide the class so that each group has an anchor to finish, and let them dig in. Later, sharing usually evokes proud smiles.

CONCLUDING OUR TEXT-BASED PROMPT

Better Answer Organizers

Next, I pull out the Answer Organizer for "Little Red Riding Hood" again (Figure 7 on page 73 and on the CD) and we revisit the prompt along with the completed Steps 1 and 2. Then, I unmask the conclusion and ask, "From what we've learned about concluding statements, what's good about this one?"

After we discuss its attributes, I invite the group to brainstorm some other possibilities. We jot down a couple to get the feel of working with text-based concluding statements and then move on to our prompt for "Goldilocks and the Three Bears." Again, we revisit the completed sections of our Answer Organizer (Figure 8 on page 75), but this time, I do not unmask the concluding statement. Instead, I invite partners to come up with some possibilities. After they've spent a while composing their ideas, we share some. Eventually, I unveil the chart's conclusion and again we assess its merits—but if your class is like mine, they'll argue that one of theirs is better than the chart's. So we'll let them use their debate steam on our other anchor charts, still devoid of conclusions. By this point, you may want to let the students select the one they'd like to finish, and then later select some to be copied onto the anchors. You'll be surprised at the results, I bet.

A Multiple-Paragraph Super Sandwich

As students mature they are expected to construct lengthier responses—ones with multiple paragraphs. This seems like a dark and looming mountain that some teachers and students hesitate to climb. Perhaps composing one good paragraph was such a monumental feat that to consider several paragraphs comes up short on positive perspectives. However, once students understand how to construct a good single paragraph with an introduction, layers of evidence, and a conclusion, mountain climbing has been made easier. Let's see why that is.

Consider first that a response with multiple paragraphs might also be a response with multiple sandwiches. Actually, when writers are having trouble developing multiple-paragraph responses, we can show them how to take a one-paragraph response and dissect it, extracting each major piece of evidence. Responders can then use those major points from the sandwich middle and reincarnate each into an introduction for a whole paragraph, rather than the minimal form each presently holds in the one-paragraph response.

Lesson II.10 on the CD takes students through this step by step using the Answer Organizer for "Goldilocks and the Three Bears." The PowerPoint slides for this Super Sandwich lesson morph the single-paragraph organizer into a multiple-paragraph organizer. These slides show students how major details in the single paragraph can be elaborated so they each require their own separate paragraph in a multiple-paragraph response. These visuals really help with this explanation. Figure 9 is the Multiple-Paragraph Super Sandwich, a visual that is also included in the PowerPoint slides for Lesson II.10 on the CD.

Using the Super Sandwich to Create a Multiple-Paragraph Self-Based Response

Now let's see how the Super Sandwich might play out using our one-paragraph, self-based body of details. We first log the key details:

1. First of all, if it's a nice day, I always go for a walk with my dog, Jesse. We have fun with our dog friends and people friends on the beach.
2. Afterward, I get busy making something interesting for supper, for example, pesto pasta or quinoa salad. Sometimes, I invite friends to join me.
3. Once the meal is over, the kitchen is clean, and the dishes are done, I figure I deserve some downtime.

4. So I check my email and watch the news.
5. I may do another chore, too, but eventually, I pick up a book I've started and enjoy reading before I finally roll back the covers and jump into bed.

Figure 9

Multiple-Paragraph Super Sandwich

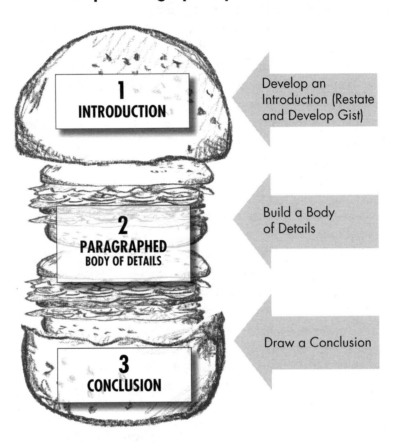

1 INTRODUCTION — Develop an Introduction (Restate and Develop Gist)

2 PARAGRAPHED BODY OF DETAILS — Build a Body of Details

3 CONCLUSION — Draw a Conclusion

Look at the first two sentences about our walk. Can you see how that can be stretched into its own paragraph by explaining more of what happens on our walk? This is also true of the other sentences. So conceivably, I could have five paragraphs sandwiched between my introduction and conclusion, which I may want to tweak a bit as well.

For example, if one of the details feels shallow—for instance number 3—I may want to combine it with another. Or I may decide to revise it a bit to make it more robust so that I can use it in a paragraph of its own. It's important to think this out aloud for the class so that they live through the stretching, revising, and reorganization through you. Please don't moan, but this part of composing will probably have to be modeled a number of times. Nobody ever said writing is easy—but we *can* make the process interesting and fun.

As a result of your demonstrations, students will understand how they, first, can develop the basic details in one paragraph—a paragraph with details upon which they can elaborate. However, they are also learning that responses can be stated in a variety of ways—and nothing here is carved in stone. But remember, *this is best accomplished through unrehearsed demonstrations.*

TEACHER SUPER SANDWICH TAWAS

There is an enormous difference between a demonstration lesson where most details are planned out and an unrehearsed demonstration. Most often, teachers are told to plan, plan, plan, if they want great lessons. However, when we plan a demonstration lesson for writing, everything turns out a bit too neat and clean and perfect. Writing is not neat and clean and perfect. Writing is usually messy and disorganized, and first efforts are sometimes pretty shabby. As a matter of fact, teachers who have seen my rough-draft messes have asked me if they could have the draft copied to use as an example for their classes.

Students need to observe a writer's messes. Real ones! They also need to see the convoluted manner in which we think our way through constructing an answer. For text-based responses, they need to observe how we go back and forth, back and forth, between the prompt, the text, and the writing. Most of all they need to hear how our minds speak to us as we do this. The best way to demonstrate this is through a think-aloud/write-aloud (TAWA) spontaneous experience.

Perhaps the best way to illustrate the entire process is through another classroom vignette. Here, I demonstrate using a TAWA that's grounded in the fairy tale "The Three Little Pigs."

Classroom Vignette

Demonstrating Steps 1, 2, and 3

"Would all of you find a seat? I have something I want to show you," Ms. Hildreth announces to her class. As the students settle into their usual spots, their teacher pulls a large blank piece of chart paper into place in front of them and places green, blue, and red markers on the nearby ledge. Scattered about the room, the seventh graders soon grow more still and quiet, ready to begin.

The teacher goes on, "Our class is getting good at responding in writing, but we can do better than good. Terrific answers take a lot of thinking. We're doing fine, but we can always strive to do better. So, today I'm going to show you something that I bet you'll enjoy."

At this point, she notices a couple of students who look at each other and then roll their eyes, so Ms. Hildreth responds, "Seriously! You'll enjoy it mainly because it'll show you that teachers also struggle in finding the right answer. We, just like you, friends, have to think about the prompt and how it relates to parts of the story—parts that could be included in our response. I had to write brief essays in that graduate class I took last semester. Ever see a teacher struggle? Just watch."

Having now gained everyone's attention, including the eye-rollers, Ms. Hildreth walks over to the board where she has posted a prompt related to the story she will use. "Today we'll work off the fairy tale 'The Three Little Pigs' again, and here is the prompt I'll be responding to. Now, notice it has several parts that we may need to address," the teacher says as she reads the prewritten prompt.

Prompt: If the First Little Pig learned his lesson in the story of "The Three Little Pigs," what materials would he use this time to build a new house?
- Why would he use these materials?
- Where might he build his new house?
- Be sure to include details from the story to support your answer.

Picking up her black marker, the teacher begins. "I'm going to circle this one and this one and this one, and you know why, right?" she asks.

"They are questions," the class responds in unison.

"Hmm. No background information. Oh, but here's a petition," she points out, circling it, "but no star because it's an implicit petition—only a reminder. We star only those that are explicit and need restating."

"Oh, that's easy," responds Maria, ready to help her teacher compose the answer.

"And, you're not struggling," admonishes Fernando.

"I'm glad you're confident, Maria! And Fernando, just be patient. You know, the reason we use fairy tales is that they help us learn the processes in a comfortable way," the teacher explains. "Today I want to introduce a demonstration technique called think-aloud and write-aloud, which is exactly what its name suggests: a lesson where I tell you—I think aloud—what's in my head.

Then, as I am writing, I am again saying aloud what I am writing or thinking. We'll call them TAWAs.

"Did you ever wonder what was in a teacher's head?" the teacher asks. "Well, you'll get to see how sometimes when I think and when I write, I get all jumbled up and have to step back or revise my thinking and my writing. At least that is what I think you'll see, because I have not practiced this, so who knows what might happen! I haven't rehearsed what I'm going to say, so you may even find it humorous that your teacher would have to go back and forth so many times. I'll probably stammer and stutter—and struggle, Fernando—so be patient and just watch, okay? Everybody ready?"

The students nod, with faces that show an interest in what is about to take place. So, Ms. Hildreth announces, "Here goes . . ." and all eyes follow her lead.

The first thing she does is read the entire prompt aloud. Then she ponders, "Let me see. I want to restate the question first, so I am writing . . . " As she speaks, she picks up the green marker and moves into a write-aloud, saying each word as she writes: "If the First Little Pig learned his lesson in the story of 'The Three Little Pigs'—now, I don't want to use *what*," she says, pointing back at the question, "because that is a question word and this is the answer. So, let's see. I could say the materials *would*—no, I don't want to say the *materials* would, I want to say the materials *he would use* this time . . . to build a new house are—no, wait. I am not sure if I want to say *are* because then I have to say more than one kind of material—plural. I kind of think the pigs would use bricks. *Is* bricks? *Are* bricks? Yes! I do want it to be *are bricks*."

Ms. Hildreth then decides to reread, "So far, I have *If the First Little Pig learned his lesson in the story of 'The Three Little Pigs,' the materials he would use to build a new house are bricks.*

"No! *Would be bricks*," she adds, revising again, and then suddenly remembering something else, she sighs, "Uh-oh, I still have the rest of the prompt to consider, so I better read to see if I want to restate anything else right now. Or maybe later in a different paragraph?"

So, the teacher again rereads the question parts. "Why would he use these materials? Where might he build his new house? Be sure to include details from the story to support your answer. Hmm. I think I should begin my next sentence with the *why* question, but I won't exactly have to restate it. Maybe . . . like . . . He would build his new house out of bricks because—yes, *why* usually goes with *because*.

"Let me read it from the beginning again and see if it sounds right. If the First Little Pig learned his lesson in the story of 'The

Three Little Pigs,' the materials he would use to build his new house would be bricks. He would build his new house out of bricks because—Okay. Why would he build his house out of bricks? 'What do you mean by this?' the Stranger would ask me.

"I'm going to jot down some things from the story on this other piece of chart paper, because I have to keep in mind that it said to use details from the story to support my answer. So-o-o-o-o . . . in the story it said that the First Pig built his first house out of straw, but then the wolf blew it in," Ms. Hildreth says as she employs a write-aloud of brief notes: *1st pig / straw / wolf blew in.*

Then, she continues to read and present through the TAWA technique: "His brother, the Second Pig, built his house out of sticks, and the wolf blew that over too." And, she writes while saying, *2nd, sticks, w. blew over.*

"So, both of those houses would not be good because they can be blown over easily," Ms. Hildreth says, moving back into a think-aloud.

"But, the Third Pig built his house out of bricks, and the wolf could not blow his house over, no matter how hard he tried," and she jots a few notes again on the chart paper: *3rd, bricks, YES! W. did not blow over!*

"Okay, but wait, the wolf could come down his chimney, so maybe the best house would have no chimney," and again at the chart she writes *Chimney = problem. No chimney?*

"Well, no . . . that wouldn't work because I think fireplaces always have to have an open hole—or do they? I don't know. So, I better not use that. But, he could put something with holes over the chimney so the smoke could get out and the wolf could not get in. Yes, I remember that when we had birds coming in our fireplace in the springtime, we had to put this wire mesh over the chimney. Then the smoke got out, but the birds couldn't come in," she says, turning to the chart again and writing: *wire over chimney?* And, thinking aloud, she reminds both the class and herself, "I won't be putting anything from my own personal experience in this, though!" Then Mrs. Hildreth turns back to her evolving response.

"Let's see . . . ," she hesitates and then rereads her incomplete answer one more time: "If the First Little Pig learned his lesson in the story of 'The Three Little Pigs,' the materials he would use to build his new house would be bricks. He would build his new house out of bricks because . . . because . . . I cannot say anything just yet about the bad straw and the bad sticks. These are details and I need a gist. I have to tell why the bricks are good. Okay . . . He would build his new house out of bricks because bricks are very strong. Yes! Good gist. I want to use details from the story, so I will write, The Third Pig built his house out of bricks because bricks are very strong. When the wolf came he could not blow it down. There! Details from the story to show that bricks are strong. But, now I'm probably going to need a transition word . . . Hmm. *Whereas?* Yes! Whereas . . . the First Pig built his house out of straw and the wolf was able to blow it right down, so straw would not be a good building material. Yes, I'm on a roll now. *Furthermore!* A great transition! Furthermore," the teacher repeats with a kind of exaggerated, elitist sophistication in her voice, "the Second Pig built his house out of sticks, and the wolf was able to blow that one down also.

"Now I think I can add the ending sentence. Oops! No! The chimney screen. Maybe I will start this one with . . . Also, he may want to make sure there is a screen or something so smoke can—No, that won't work because the sentence will be too long. Let me see. Also, he may want to make sure there is . . . is . . . something on the chimney hole . . . to let the smoke out, but . . . but, but, keep the wolf from getting in.

"Okay. The paragraph conclusion. I'm going to look back at the first part and restate it again—use that circular technique. Let's see. I think I could write, That is why the First Pig would choose bricks this time. Good!" And she reaches for her red marker and begins writing as she repeats: "That is why—Good ending!

"Now, I'll read that whole paragraph over to make sure it sounds right." Ms. Hildreth goes on to reread the paragraph, and just as she thinks she is finished, she exclaims, "Oh, my gosh! Wait. I'm not done because there is another part to the question: Where might he build his new house? I better restate that new question and—uh-oh—start a whole new paragraph, because I just ended the last one. Yikes! It's a good thing they gave me a whole page of space.

"So here we go again. The First Pig might build his new house—Where? Where would he build it? Use story details—where did the others build their houses? Well, they were close enough that they could run to each other's houses when they were in trouble. But, when they ran to the Third Pig's house it sounded like they just made it. Maybe I should have them live really close together. It said I had to use details from the story and there weren't many details about where they built their houses. There weren't any pictures, either. Maybe I could answer using those few details the author did give, and then at the very end add only one other sentence that would come from my own head about where a good place would be.

Just to add a touch of voice right at the end. But, I will have to be careful because the person who made up this question wants me to use only details from the story."

So, the teacher grabs her green marker and continues to write aloud. "The First Pig might build his new house . . . he might build his new house . . . close to the other two pigs—No, too detailed for a gist. I'm going to say . . . " (and the teacher strikes out the last six words) "close to his family. Yes! Too many pig words in here!" she says, and giving a little snort, glances over her glasses at the class with a smirk that invites humor into the moment.

"Okay, so now I have to explain why living near family is important. Back to details from the story. The First Pig might build his new house close to his family," Ms. Hildreth rereads. "I'm not going to put a *because* this time. I'll save the supporting details for the very next sentence instead. The First Pig might build his new house close to his family. When the wolf almost caught him and his brother, they ran to the next house to be safe. Okay. So what? They ran to the next house. So what? the Stranger would ask. If the next house had been farther away, the wolf would have caught them. Connecting word. Connecting word? *Therefore*, the First Pig would build his house very close to—Use a synonym. Say family in a different way. Therefore, the First Pig would build his house close to . . . those who love him and . . . and, and . . . I've got it! They will take care of him if he gets into trouble, just like the Third Little Pig did. Good! Now. An ending for this paragraph . . . and maybe for the whole thing." She then trades in her blue marker for a red one.

"Let's see. I'll go back and reread the key question again before I decide how to end this. If the First Little Pig learned his lesson in the story of 'The Three Little Pigs,' what materials would he use this time to build a new house? Why would he use these materials?

"Well . . . maybe I will add just a touch of my own opinion here at the end—but not too much. Just enough to add some voice to this writing," she thinks aloud and then goes on into a TAWA: "I hope that both the First Pig and the Second Pig did learn their lesson because . . . because . . . because . . . if they did not . . . they may not live to . . . to . . . to . . . to tell the tale again. Yes! That's good!" the teacher exclaims and then rereads the whole sentence: "I hope that both the First Pig and the Second Pig did learn their lesson because if they did not they may not live to tell the tale again. But, I don't want a one-sentence paragraph, so I can either move it up into the last paragraph or add more. I guess maybe I will just move it up to conclude the last paragraph and see how that feels."

At this point, the teacher rereads the questions and then the entire piece aloud, eliminates a couple of words, then turns to the group, and asks, "Questions? Comments?"

Several students respond by suggesting what she could have added to the piece. The teacher agrees with them, but later explains, "You know, there are a million correct ways this could have been written. I'm glad you have good ideas too. I'll let you use your own ideas on a new one tomorrow. We'll do buddy-sharing and you can do a TAWA from the new question with your partners. Like what I did with you today. But, right now it is time for lunch!"

It is really quite amazing how students are scaffolded forward through this kind of think-aloud/write-aloud experience. Yet, it should not be so surprising that when we make covert processes overt, students readily learn them, because we let the secret out of the bag.

OOPS! WE AREN'T THERE YET!

It would seem that once we have students to this point in the response journey, the process is complete. After all, we have worked through all three steps. But this is not usually the case, because there are important postwriting suggestions that should also be addressed. First of all, every piece of writing should be reread.

Undoubtedly, there are multiple reasons to reread. Yet it's tough getting writers to do it—even adult writers. Therefore, our best hope is to engrain it as a habit, an actual piece of the process. It's actually a postprocess assessment piece, because we reread to assess.

But how do we assess? What tools do we use? Part III of this book will answer not only those questions, but many more that may arise—especially if you're working with struggling students.

POSTWRITING:
ASSESSMENT AND
OUR RESPONSE TO IT

CHAPTER 7

GETTING STARTED WITH ASSESSMENT AND ITS RESPONSE

I'll tell you a secret: Most young writers don't reread what they've written.
They skip over that all-important step.
—Ralph Fletcher, *How Writers Work:*
Finding a Process That Works for You

It might appear to many educators that the purpose of today's assessments is reporting—reporting to students, parents, the district, the state, and now even the federal government. Sometimes it seems like maybe education has lost sight of the primary purpose of assessment, that is, assessing to inform instruction. *We assess in order to respond, and we respond in order to better assist each learner in becoming all that he or she might be.*

DIALOGUE: THE KEY TO PROGRESS

Optimally, such response occurs through dialogues—dialogues that can involve others besides the teacher. Peers can collaborate and respond to each other's writing; teacher aides, assistants, and specialists can respond; classroom volunteers can lend a hand (or an ear); and parents, given a little guidance, can also respond. Plus, many schools now have technology that allows for email dialoguing between teachers and students. Regardless, for an assessment to be meaningful, it needs to be followed by a related dialogue.

Without that postassessment dialogue, the time spent assessing all those papers may be for naught. How many students will pensively ponder your assessment? How many will understand their areas of need and work to improve those areas the next time around? How many will even understand *how* to improve? Yes, assessing a stack of responses to sample test prompts can lead the teacher toward classroom lessons, but student progress is usually slow when individual needs are not analyzed and discussed.

So let's move away from yesteryear's assign-collect-correct habit. Don't let the buck stop with correcting. Decide early on: With whom can this student dialogue about my assessment of his or her writing? You see, the assessment itself represents a very minimal kind of right-wrong response, more related to accountability than to student support. Learners need more than assessment. They need assessments that come with response dialogues.

That is why this final, postwriting section of *Better Answers* combines assessment and our response to it. For the best results, teachers use both.

STUDENTS AS SELF-EVALUATORS

I've mentioned teacher assessment, but actually, the students themselves should be the first assessors of the pieces they produce. To do this, they must reread their writing. And the Better Answer Rubric (see Figure 10 and the CD) can lead them to do this successfully.

Because the Better Answer protocol is structured, the Better Answer Rubric can follow in its footsteps. This means that after students learn each step of the process, it is indeed the qualities of that step that are examined in the assessment. It comes as no surprise to the students, then, when the rubric asks whether they've restated the question, developed a gist, built a body of details, and so forth. However, the rubric also includes a few other important assessment areas, such as neatness and writing conventions. Its simplicity helps both students and teachers, as well as anyone else lending a hand in the assessment process. Furthermore, it can be used across subject areas.

Students need to know—even before they begin to write—that the assessment tool being used aligns with the protocol they've been taught. Knowing

Better Answer
Rubrics and Scales

this, they'll feel confident that, if they explicitly follow the protocol, they will probably do well on the assessment. This is important, because all too often in school students have no idea of how their work will be assessed.

So before kids begin to write, we want them to understand that, once they've put the final mark at the end of their last sentence, they should immediately reread to assess, using this Better Answer Rubric.

Figure 10

The Better Answer Rubric

Name _____ Date _____

	Minimally 1	Partially 2	Completely 3
Restates question in the answer	_____	_____	_____
Develops a gist answer	_____	_____	_____
Uses details to support the answer	_____	_____	_____
Draws conclusion	_____	_____	_____
Stays on topic	_____	_____	_____
Writes neatly	_____	_____	_____
Uses proper conventions	_____	_____	_____

SHARED ASSESSMENT GROUNDS INDEPENDENT ASSESSMENT

This scale is simplistic and thus lends itself to easy use. Nevertheless, students still need support in using the rubric *before* they use it independently. For example, invite the class to analyze anonymous pieces of writing using the Better Answer Rubric. You can begin with some of the examples of student writing on the CD. Simply display a sample response along with the Better Answer Rubric in chart form, then invite discussion.

There's much more on student assessment and response experiences in the next two chapters—which is good because the more students assess, the better they'll be at analyzing, revising, and editing their own pieces, as well as those of their peers. Every year, I can predict that until my students begin assessing their own writing, improvement will be slow. For it is when they come to see

their own writing through the eyes of others that everything begins to gel. And that's just another reason why assessment dialogues are so important.

THE IMPORTANCE OF HUMAN DIALOGUE DURING THE PROCESS

All too often we give students practice in responding to prompts and we assess their responses, but with a mountain of multiple mandates before us, we stop there. We don't actually *use* each assessment as a tool for response. Sometimes we do ask the students to revise or edit their work, after which they return the work to us for a second assessment. However, without any teacher-student dialogue related to that first assessment, students have a tough time improving on the original. So someone should dialogue with them about the areas needing attention. It can be the teacher, or it can be another student, a parent, or a classroom aide. Obviously, the best pathway would involve the teacher; however, there isn't always time in a jam-packed day for that. Yet the improvement will be slow and halted unless another human being is involved in that assessment-and-response process.

A RESPONSE AVENUE FOR EACH ASSESSMENT

"Good grief!" you exclaim. "For every assessment? How can I possibly respond every time I hand back a corrected written response?"

Remember—you, the teacher, do *not* have to be the one to respond. As I mentioned, others are able to dialogue with a student about an assessment he or she has received. But there is a way that a teacher can be a part of the dialogue, even when he or she is unable to be there physically.

SOME TIPS FOR IMPLEMENTING RESPONSE AFTER ASSESSMENT

By jotting a few notes on the assessment form, a teacher can focus its related dialogue in a positive direction. That's what I ask teachers to do when I meet with their students one-on-one. That is, I suggest that they mark the Better Answer Rubric, adding a bit of narrative to focus my intentions. It works like a charm and keeps us all on the same page.

Teachers write their intentions, but they also often take me aside for two seconds to whisper a guideline in my ear before I move to dialogue with a student. Mary Manning, a fourth-grade teacher, did this when I consulted in her classroom recently. She whispered, "The prompt asked them to write a letter. I cannot believe how many responded nicely, but forgot to use letter form. Please focus on that!" So I did.

You can see from this example how important it is that anyone who is going to respond to a student's writing be privy not only to the teacher's assessment, but also to the prompt. If the prompt is located in some obscure spot, be sure to copy it for assessment use. After all, how can an assessor know if the writer restated the prompt unless the prompt is right there to examine? I might add that the teacher would also need the prompt when taking responses home to correct. *Just remember to keep the prompt handy throughout the process.*

Even in peer-to-peer response dialogues, those brief teacher comments help. Besides merely checking each descriptor on the Better Answer Rubric, the teacher jots a few words or questions to get a dialogue started. That way, peer-to-peer discussion will grow out of the teacher's intentions, and the two heads—along with the teacher's comments—just may come up with ways to improve a product.

It makes sense, then, to plan how such person-to-person interactions can take place. I've learned over years of working with writers that their primary need is just to have someone listen as they read their writing. The more writers read to a responsive listener, the more they will revise to make it better, the more they'll think about it, and the faster they will come to understand the meaning of audience—to see their own writing through another's eyes.

I know you'll be surprised at how rapidly the class internalizes the Better Answers protocol and how student listeners notice where tweaks are needed in another student's writing. Using the Better Answers Rubric and the assessment tools and ideas in the next chapter will support the process. And for adults who want to help more but don't know how, the final chapter of this book should be a great support, because it gives suggestions for "what to do when . . . " It's a handy reference to keep close by.

So one way or another, decide on student dialogue avenues that can be accessed so that writers have human beings who can (at least) listen to their finished responses. Ideally, there will be those who can mindfully use the ideas and tools in the next two chapters to guide the writer toward success.

This Postwriting "Getting Started" chapter has emphasized how assessment and our response to it are inseparable and crucial to a student's progress in constructing responses. Along with assessment tools that align with the process, such as the Better Answer Rubric, students can learn how to assess their own writing and help others in the process. Yet, in order to do this, they need lots of related experiences. The following two chapters can lead the way.

CHAPTER 8

CONSTRUCTIVE
ASSESSMENT

*Conferring well with students requires that I have a vision of what I hope for
them as writers. Just as listening up close has everything to do with how to confer,
stepping back to see the big picture is equally important.*
— Joanne Hindley, *In the Company of Children*

My mom used to tell me, "You can catch more bees with honey than with
vinegar." It's a metaphor related to positive reinforcement—a sweetness that
works wonders.

That's why I always tell the kids, "I'm looking for reasons to celebrate."
Lots of points to glow on! *Just one to grow on!* When I look over a student's
shoulder, I find everything I possibly can to celebrate. After that positive reinforcement brings me into relationship with that student, only then do I slide
gently into one suggestion to grow on. My main intent is always: Leave 'em

smiling. After all, learning isn't as serious as we sometimes make it out to be. It's fun! It's a celebration! So find all those reasons to celebrate.

Creating Positive Perspectives

During those stolen moments when we confer with individual students, we may not realize it, but each move we make models something for those around us. That is, students see how we do it, and then they follow suit. If we always begin by asking, "Do you know what I notice about this that makes me want to celebrate (or impresses me)?" it nudges everyone to use that same pleasant entree. And it doesn't matter how insignificant those points noticed might be. For example, I might celebrate, "Look at the way you indented the beginning of your paragraph. You are definitely looking good in indenting!" or "I love the way you used that word! I would never have thought to use it that way" or "You always space your words so nicely so that I can easily read each one. How do you manage that, anyway?" Quite simply, we develop a wide variety of reasons to celebrate, and it is these that become a driving force to success.

Furthermore, amidst all this good-news sharing, there's a lot of learning going on, because others in the class hear and grow from it. Plus, no one's afraid or intimidated when the news is almost all good. As a matter of fact, others sit eagerly awaiting a turn to hear their good news—as they work to make certain their own writing possesses some of those same reasons to celebrate.

Even now, when I volunteer to do one-on-one conferring at a nearby school, the teacher tells me that the kids can't wait to have their turn with Ms. Cole—maybe because I leave 'em smiling. If I help kids feel good about their relationship with me *and* their relationship with writing, they'll love to write. And anything we love, we usually do well. Bottom line: Offer responders a pound of celebrations and an ounce of next-time suggestions—and I guarantee you'll leave 'em smiling.

WHAT'S BEING ASSESSED?

Published authors tend to assess every piece of writing that comes our way—no matter where we might encounter it. Whether it's an environmental editorial or a book review or a persuasive letter, we investigate not only its subject, but also its style, tone, form, and conventions. We carefully consider each genre, each purpose. This is what we want kids to do.

We can begin by revisiting the Boundaries Scale. And now that the students have the Better Answer protocol under their belts, we can analyze each piece of writing using the Better Answer Rubric. We begin by finding a variety of similar pieces, which we assess together. But these pieces come from *outside* our classroom.

I never display a class member's response so others can observe, analyze, and assess it. I've had teachers say that they first ask a student if it's okay—which is fine *as long as we're focused on celebrating*. But we put our students in a very vulnerable spot when we start evaluating their work in front of others. You see, kids innocently volunteer, predicting that we will celebrate their wonderful writing—but that feeling dissipates within an atmosphere of open and unpredictable response, leaving the authors less than they were.

However, we can indeed assess others' responses, but let's use anonymous responses from outside the classroom. The Web is chockfull of examples—both school-related and life-related. Just hop onto a state website and check to see if that state offers benchmarked examples. States such as New York, Ohio, Washington, and Kentucky will make your job a lot easier. What's more, go to www.amazon.com and gather a few book reviews (some will make your neediest writers look good). Or go to the "Hot Toys" section on the Consumer Reports website (www.consumerreports.org) for a few responses related to toys, games, or technology. And blogs are full of responses, but be sure to read before using. You can analyze and discuss everything from Web examples, because they aren't written by students in your class, so do a little surfing and fill your assessment coffers.

Assessment: Better Answer Tools and Interventions

Right at the beginning of the Better Answer process, I encouraged that, prior to beginning this process, a preinstruction assessment be done. Then, throughout each chapter, I offered ongoing (formative) Assessment-Conferring sections—ideas that were pertinent to that particular step in the process, as well as suggestions for using certain tools or tactics. But now, with all this under our belts, we can finally make use of the Better Answer Rubric.

The Better Answer Rubric works well as a response-to-intervention (RtI) tactic, because after teachers (or students) use it, they'll know what areas in the Better Answer protocol require more instruction and support. If a student scores poorly in Restates the Question or Petition on the rubric, the teacher simply returns to the related suggestions in that chapter of this book as well as to the ideas offered in Chapter 9, "What to Do When . . . : Responding to Assessment." Even paraprofessionals, such as teacher aides and assistants, will understand the direction for instruction.

MONITORING RESPONSE PROGRESS ACROSS THE SUBJECT AREAS

The Better Answer Rubric can be used for all subjects. Don't be surprised, though, if students' performance differs from one subject to the next. Because the content differs, Sal may do far better in science response writing than in literature. Yet, because the rubric can be a common tool used across subject areas, it helps us better understand whether poor response scores in one subject area are related to difficulty with writing or that subject's content.

KEEP IT SIMPLE

The Better Answer Rubric helps you keep it simple, because once students internalize the rubric, they'll be able to instantly assess their own writing. Plus, it allows you to easily highlight all the good things that are happening in a piece as well as that one area to grow on. In the beginning, I usually circumvent the sandwich middle as a target area. I focus on celebrating things like exact-word-match restating, general gist answers, adequate spacing, and readable handwriting. And as for my intervention target, I make certain it's a doable one. Baby steps.

Then when a student is claiming 3s in these easier areas, I slide my scaffolding into the sandwich middle—but just one aspect in that sandwich middle, please. For example, you might discuss a response's organization, suggesting that the writer cut apart (with scissors) his key facts to see if they'd work better in another order. "Play with it a bit," I'd suggest in this case, trying not to sound like, "This is wrong! Do it over!" Besides, those of us who write to publish will tell you, honestly, that we spend hours and hours playing with our writing. Playing is a good thing! (Don't get me wrong, though—there are also long hours when I keep my nose to the grindstone.)

A THREE-POINT SCALE

Many teachers ask, "Why did you use a three-point scale?" My answer: "To keep it simple." Today's students and teachers are inundated with rubrics for every subject, some of which are very complex. Such rubrics may be necessary; however, for our purpose here, this three-point scale works like a charm. Students know that they are either doing it, almost doing it, or minimally doing it. Simple. Plus, teachers aren't sitting around deliberating over all the descriptors in a six-point scale.

When students omit one of the Better Answer attributes (for instance, they do not restate the question at all), I simply leave that area blank on their rubric.

In this way, if they revise their answer, I can then fill in a score. Teachers who prefer a four-point scale can simply extend the scoring levels to include a 0, the score for students who demonstrate no evidence in a given area.

ASSESSING FOR ANSWER SANDWICH ATTRIBUTES: CONTENT AND READABLENESS

The scale has two major sections: content and readableness. It's easy to see that the first four areas on the Better Answer Rubric replicate Steps 1, 2, and 3 in the Better Answer Protocol, which relate to *content*. Stays on Topic is an organizational nudge that also deals with the content of the writing.

However, Writes Neatly and Uses Proper Conventions describe a response's *readableness*. That is, do the responder's neatness, spelling, grammar, and other conventions make it easy or difficult for us to read the piece? In the end, both content and readableness can make or break a response.

MONITORING PROGRESS USING DATA SPREADSHEETS

It was really helpful when I was a literacy coach to keep a class spreadsheet on which I logged all students along the vertical axis and the seven parts of the Better Answer Rubric along the horizontal. I could quickly check it when grouping students for a mini-lesson or any other time I needed a quick reference. For example, when a teacher or parent wanted to know how a particular student was progressing, my spreadsheet offered us up-to-date information. This book's CD contains some templates of spreadsheets we used: the Class Monitoring Spreadsheet and the Individual Student Monitoring Spreadsheet.

We can actually use the spreadsheets' data as part of our value-added assessment portfolio that monitors individual student growth. But the data also will show those who have a common area of need. What's more, they can be used across grade levels and subjects. In other words, they're handy resources.

MONITORING USING PROGRESS PORTFOLIOS

A progress folder is one of the most informative aspects of the entire assessment repertoire. Each portfolio or folder holds samples of student work. Onto each sample is stapled a marked Better Answer Rubric, offering an at-a-glance assessment of every response sample. The students and I select monthly pieces of work to demonstrate growth, then place the sample into their folders. Later, I can access that portfolio to log results on my spreadsheet or for any other purpose for which I might need a sample of progress. Furthermore, when a student needs a positive perk, I pull out his or her progress sheet and show the continual progress. Like magic, attitudinal wounds heal, and he or she is back in writing mode before I have a chance to refile the folder.

WHO'S ASSESSING?

As I mentioned earlier, assessment and its related response have moved beyond the auspices of only the teacher. We now feel that students themselves should have a solid grasp of the assessment-response process. Let's see how we can help make that happen.

STUDENT SELF-ASSESSMENT: REREADING THE RESPONSE WITH THE BETTER ANSWER RUBRIC IN MIND

One of the primary reasons writers must not forget to reread is because even professional writers make silly mistakes; they omit words or write words twice, overuse a particular word, and forget the value of transitions. Rereading allows us to fix our faux pas. But reading a piece in its entirety, which many forget to do, also opens a responder's ears to its disorganization, its lack of flow, its missing pieces, and other problems.

Reread to a Partner

Rereading a finished response is imperative. And one sure way to lead students toward that habit is to ask them to read their completed response to someone else, inviting the listener to initial the back page. Between the two heads, they usually uncover most obvious problems. Plus, the connected chat scaffolds both to a higher level of performance. Once they see the value of rereading, students begin to *automatically* read everything over.

Sign Off

Another easy method to make certain that students reread their responses is to use a simple checklist, which they sign and hand in with their completed responses. (See Figure 11 and the CD.)

Figure 11

Response Sign-Off Checklist

_____ I found all of the petitions and questions in the prompt.
_____ I restated all petitions and questions.
_____ I constructed a gist in my introduction.
_____ I found details to use as evidence.
_____ I found ways to insert some smart transitions.
_____ I developed a conclusion.
_____ I reread my response from beginning to end.
_____ I am happy with my response now.

Initials_____ Date_____

PEER COLLABORATION: DEFENDING A RESPONSE USING THE BETTER ANSWER RUBRIC

I begin collaborative peer assessment by asking the responders to score their pieces using the Better Answer Rubric, and afterward, meet with a partner to defend those scores by locating each piece of evidence. In this process, students should actually point out their restated words or take their partners back into the text to the supporting section. This technique works like magic.

But I have to demonstrate this process the first couple of times using my own writing so that students can follow my lead. Without teacher modeling, students will respond in myriad ways, which may or may not be supportive. So, modeling is mandatory here.

I might begin by using a familiar piece, such as one from a previous TAWA. I run through each part of the Better Answer Rubric and explain my reasoning for each part as it relates to my response. I begin with, "I restated the question because the question was . . . and I used the following words from the prompt . . . I gave a gist answer for the question because I said . . . and that answer was not specific, but still gave the main idea." I carry on in the same fashion through the other parts of the rubric. Please try to fit in several of these demonstrations before asking students to defend their own responses.

To simplify matters, I use some past responses from an old state assessment. After several of these demonstrations, partners are ready to collaborate.

As partners share their own responses with each other in a similar fashion, I tour the room, scaffolding along the way. Note that after sharing with a partner, students should be offered a period of time in which to edit or revise. It's

important they have this revision opportunity; otherwise, they tend to stop midstream to insert omitted words, erase spelling errors, and the like, which of course bores the listener and usurps an inordinate amount of time. During the share, they can mark the edit spots, but save the actual editing for later.

TEACHER CONFERRING: USING THE BETTER ANSWER TOOLS

Author Stephen King, in his memoir *On Writing* (2000), reveals that the individual who helped him the most in his writing was newspaper editor John Gould for whom he worked during high school. First, the editor marked King's columns using editing marks. Then, with King beside him, Gould addressed each mark, but explained only those King did not understand. This kind of data-driven conferring sure seems like it would work with our students too.

And, as I mentioned earlier, conferring that's guided by the Better Answer Rubric and its related spreadsheets can be used as a kind of nonstandardized *value-added assessment*, because the data offer the means through which we can monitor individual and group assessment data, establish patterns of growth or need, and compare students' growth across time. Plus, spreadsheets that hold this longitudinal data can be utilized across all subject areas that use constructed-response assessment. Thus, the Better Answer Rubric and the monitoring spreadsheets guide teachers toward data-driven decision-making.

ASSESSING ♦ CONFERRING

ASSESSMENT TYPE: **The Better Answer Rubric**

Students are now ready to make steady use of this scale across the curriculum. If the class is having a health test on which one part asks that they explain how the stomach digests food, we expect them to transfer the Better Answer protocol to that performance task. To emphasize this across-the-day use, we usually staple a (reduced, quarter-page) Better Answer Rubric to the corner of each response page beforehand. In that way, it becomes a visible nudge for constructing a sound answer. The mark they receive on the rubric is usually logged as a language arts score.

FOCUS QUESTIONS

Questions from the answer scale drive both the assessment and the conferring sessions. Afterward, when meeting with individual students, we often work from their corrected papers (with the rubric attached). We focus on positive points first, and then end the conference with one rubric area that needs improvement as well as a possible strategy to bring this about.

Revisiting the Preinstruction Responses

Now it's time to dig that pile of preinstruction, baseline assessments from your coffers and mark each using the Better Answer Rubric. Afterward, match each student's pre- and postassessments and growth. Then pat yourself on the back—and the students too. It's time to celebrate!

Saving Time

After the students have the Better Answer protocol under their belts, I confer in a way that conserves time. For example, if the students have responded to a reading prompt, I take those papers home, staple a quarter-page copy of the Better Answer Rubric to each one, and mark it accordingly. I can also use margin marks to further direct students. Within the next few days (so that my aging mind does not lose track), I call each student over for a five-minute conference (set a timer if need be), focusing first on their 3s, that is, what they did well, and then on one (just *one*) area in which I feel they can improve. But I always try to leave them smiling.

Better Answer
Rubrics and Scales

Exit Commitments

It works best to zero in on the easiest-to-accomplish areas first, after which I offer my one piece of advice. But before they leave my side, I ask the following *very important question*: "The next time you construct a response, what will you do differently?"

Each of their answers becomes an exit commitment. It gives the teacher an instructional focus, and it gives the student a specific goal for improvement. You might even want them to note those commitments in writing. This worked so well that when I was a literacy coach conferring with students in Barb McKay's fourth grade, she said, "Ardie! I can't believe how the kids remember their exit commitments. They all know what they need to do better next time!"

What About the Tough Cases?

There's one thing we teachers learn early on: There will always be tough cases. But as long as students follow the Better Answer protocol, they will have at least the bare bones of a response—and from bare bones we can build and build and build. The assessment tools and techniques in this chapter and throughout the book will guide you and your students toward better answers. Yet, when you wear thin and don't know what to do next, I bet you just may find the answer in the next chapter in this book. So read on.

CHAPTER 9

WHAT TO DO WHEN . . . : RESPONDING TO ASSESSMENT

When the going gets tough, the tough get going.
—Joseph P. Kennedy

After a few years of classroom experience, we teachers usually manage to "fly by the seat of our pants" through most instructional challenges. We learn to adjust our methods in order to produce the best results. However, there are still times when we get stuck and don't know which way to turn. At times like those, when your brain wears thin on ideas, surf through this chapter for help. It's full of tactics that might point you in an encouraging direction when you just can't think of what to do next.

Each heading that follows focuses on what is sometimes a troublesome teaching area, such as "When Responders Have Trouble Introducing a Response." Then, right after each problem, I offer a suggestion or two or three.

Sometimes you'll want to mimic the suggestions lock, stock, and barrel. At other times, the suggestions may offer just enough to get your mind going in a more productive direction. Either way, two heads are often better than one. So keep this chapter tabbed for quick reference.

WHEN RESPONDERS HAVE TROUBLE INTRODUCING A RESPONSE

Offer Practice Restating

When I first dove into this process in the 1990s, there was nothing on the Web. Now it's full of resources that lend themselves to this part of the process. For example, to locate both prompts and sample responses, you can use your own state website or click on some of the live links for other states. Students think it's interesting when you let them know the samples you're using come from a different state. Just ask dyads to take turns restating all kinds of prompts. And if you're lucky, you'll locate some that align with your own curriculum. You can even invite the students to evaluate the content of the prompts themselves.

Invite the Students into the Teacher's Role

After students use some teacher-constructed prompts, it's fun for them to create some of their own. The Better Questions Menu (Figure 3 and the CD) and the Petition Framework (Figure 2 and the CD) give students a broad range of question and petition options. Invite them to use those terms to create a prompt from known fairy tales and fables. Afterward, they can share with a partner, constructing restatements to each other's questions.

Often, partners don't stop with the restatement, but instead, roll right into the answer, because they feel so confident. When I hear someone flow from the restatement right on into the answer, however—to add a spark of levity—I dash over and make a referee time-out sign with my hands, usually accompanied by, "No, no, no! No answers! Just restatements!" which draws a giggle or two; underneath it all I would speculate that they are thinking, "A teacher who doesn't want answers!"

Afterward, with their restatements in hand, they enjoy changing partners (much like a television game show) to guess what the petition or question might have been when given only the constructed restatements. Keeping tasks playful and easy is important. It captures the students' interest and grounds the process in a positive perspective, which recent brain research informs us dramatically boosts learning (Begley 2007).

Offer Practice Constructing Introductions

Once students have experience creating prompts, this activity can be used as a postreading activity. (Just toss that reading comprehension ditto and use this instead.) Ask students to develop six good text-related prompts that will be shared with a reading buddy: three petitions and three questions. When they finish, they can trade with a partner, who will then restate the question or petition and develop a gist for each prompt. That is, partners will fulfill Step 1 of the protocol.

When they're finished, they can let either their partner or the teacher check those restatements. Regardless, I guarantee that students will not only better digest the text they've read, they will also enjoy the task more.

Teach Common Introductory Gists After Closed Restatements

Sometimes when they use a closed restatement, responders feel bewildered as to how to approach the gist. To make certain their introduction points them in the right direction, I advise kids to give the gist a sentence of its own and offer the following examples (along with their prompt and closed restatement):

Common Gist Starters (Related to *Charlie and the Chocolate Factory* by Ronald Dahl)
Prompt: Describe the kind of person Charlie's grandpa was. Use information from the story to support your answer.
Closed Restatement: Charlie's grandpa seemed to be loving and thoughtful.
Gist Starters:
- There are several reasons for this that explain this/why this is so.
- Let me explain how/why/when . . .
- You'll find the following provides evidence for my thinking/why this is so.
- Here are some ideas that support my perspective.
- Here's why/how/where.
- My response helps explain this.
- Allow me to explain why this is so/how this happens.
- Let me offer you several sound reasons as evidence.

Other Charts and Visuals

These probably sound familiar, because many of the expository pieces we read (news articles, public petitions, etc.) are woven with these words. Not only do these gist starters work, but don't they also sound smart? Many common gist introductions possess a quantitative nature, so I've made a Quantitative Gist Chart, which you can post for handy reference.

Offer Practice in Discerning Detailed and General Gists

It's fun and fast to present students with a whole raft of prompts along *with* their gist and non-gist answers; then, quickly invite the group to decide which are and which are not gist answers. Again, this works best when related to the curriculum and can even serve as a source of review or study.

To begin, the students should have a piece of poster board on which they have printed "Gist" on one side and "Detailed" on the other. When the teacher finishes reading or projecting a prompt along with its restatement and possible gist answer, students display either "Gist" or "Detailed." For example, if the class is studying a unit on space, the teacher might use this prompt for the gists that follow it:

> *Prompt:* Why do we need to wear special clothing in outer space?
> 1. We need to wear special clothing in outer space because the conditions are not like those on Earth. (Gist)
> 2. We need to wear special clothing in outer space because it is too cold and there is no air. (Detailed)

After this and a few other similar examples, have students create their own unit assessment prompts and both types of answers for the prompts. There's even a possibility that some of theirs could be used in a repeat performance on their unit test. Imagine giving a test on which students, themselves, have generated the prompts!

Invite Self-Evaluations of Completed Response Introductions

I recently spent an hour one morning asking fourth graders to read their introductions to me. Those who had sound gist statements directed toward the big picture seemed to complete their writing task competently. Those who had weak introductions had weak compositions. In other words, that introduction is really a crucial piece.

But students need tons of experience evaluating introductions in order to be able to judge their own. I offer some examples below, and the CD has more. Display a prompt alongside each of the introductions. Partners then (1)

discuss whether the introduction presents a restatement of the prompt and (2) whether its gist is indeed general. That is, it bears no details that should be kept for evidence, yet it provides a main idea. Afterward, ask partners to number the examples from best to poorest. Such comparisons provoke discussion and depth of critical thought.

Other Charts and Visuals

Paragraph Introductions, Good or Poor?

Use real prompts from the community or school newspaper and develop a set of response introductions, some of which are poor, whereas others are quite good. Ask partners to evaluate, and then later move into a whole-class share.

Prompt: More and more bikers are using the roads in our town. Some people have suggested we develop bike paths for the bikers. Write to the town board and tell them whether you want bike trails. Be sure to explain reasons for your thinking.

Introductions:
Dear Board Member,

   I agree with the people who are suggesting bike paths for our town. Here's why I feel bike paths would help make our town safer and healthier.

Dear Board Members,

   I like bike paths because they are fun. I have a new bike to ride on bike paths.

Dear Board Members,

   I think the idea of constructing bike trails for bikers is a good one. Let me offer you several sound reasons why I think bike trails would help our community.

Dear Board Member,

   I've read that the town is thinking about making bike paths, and I think this is a good idea. Bike paths help us exercise and stay healthy. They give us someplace safe to ride a bike. Plus, our moms won't have to worry about us so much. Let me explain why I want bike paths for our town.

Dear Board Member,

   Do you ride a bike? I do. That's why I want bike paths for our town. I cannot believe that anyone who rides a bike would not want bike paths. If you do not ride a bike, maybe you don't want bike paths. However, I hope you get a bike soon.

WHEN RESPONDERS NEED SUPPORT DEVELOPING DETAILS AND EVIDENCE

Other Charts and Visuals

Use a Graphic Organizer from the Petition Framework

The Petition Framework (see Figure 2 on page 27 and the CD) offers students a head start in developing evidence for their sandwich middle. Its directive petition terms point responders toward a better answer pathway. For example, if students are asked to "evaluate," they know they can organize their thinking with a T-chart, placing pros on one side and cons on the other. Then, as they revisit the text or the subject, they can judge each fact, placing it in its appropriate column. They then possess the main points on which they can elaborate. Thus, the T-chart allows them to sort and order—and perhaps best of all, that kind of edge on the process helps develop a writer's confidence. Besides, we know that each of us can often use a good start to get us going.

Use a Picture Grid

You've heard it said that a picture is worth a thousand words. This is especially true for young children who prefer to draw rather than write. So let's use drawing to open writing's coffers. I've used this technique a ton of times and it works like a charm. So please, try it.

Ask students to fold a large piece of paper in half two times, which upon unfolding reveals four rectangles. Suggest that they draw a picture of the beginning of their explanation, narrative, or description in Box 1 (the upper left). For example, suppose they've been asked to describe why the bears were angry at Goldilocks. In Box 1 they might show Goldilocks breaking into the bears' house or maybe Goldilocks eating Mama Bear's porridge.

After that first box (which is usually pretty easy) I ask them to move to the last box and draw the very end of the explanation, story, or description. In the Goldilocks example, they'd perhaps draw the bed breaking or Goldilocks running away.

When responders have the beginning and the end, it is far easier to fill in the two middle pictures. Once they possess all of the pictures, we move into dyads, where they can explain each picture to their partner (rehearsal for writing). Later, they can develop a caption for each picture. It then takes but a small effort to turn those captions into the expected paragraph form.

For more involved responses, ask students to fold papers three or four times. I usually also ask that they draw a line across the bottom of each box to save room for its caption. However, it is still best to do the first and last box before the rest, because it stretches their thinking. (I've done this with first grade and I've done it with struggling middle school students. Trust me—it works.)

Turn On Your Mind's TV

When kids get stuck right off the bat, strategies in visualization really help move the process along. I give students these directions: "Close your eyes and turn on your mind TVs. Now switch to the channel with the beginning of the story [event, situation, or such]. Where are you? What's it like there? What's happening?" After a bit, I reiterate each of those questions and suggest they turn to a partner and answer. As you may already be predicting, the next step is drawing.

It's interesting how this technique works for struggling learners. Those TVs! Sometimes they *are* handy devices (but not often).

In Text-Based Writing Skim for Details

During my nine years as a literacy coach, I ran into many students who had no idea how to skim for specific details. Instead, for every single question or petition, they would begin at the beginning and plow through each word, each sentence, each paragraph. This is not a good strategy. First, it consumes an inordinate amount of time, which finds many students caught short. Plus, it's boring to keep reading the same thing over and over. So let's teach skimming.

If the text possesses headings and subheadings, we can begin by showing students how to let those be our guide. If it doesn't, students can be taught to slide their finger down the side of the page, pulling their eyes quickly through the print in search of key terms. Another possibility is to simply read the first sentence of each paragraph, which should offer its main idea. Obviously, these are reading, not writing, tactics; yet, an inability to skim will take its toll on their ability to write.

Leave It In or Leave It Out: Marking Important Details

A key comprehension strategy involves discerning important from unimportant details (Harvey and Goudvis 2007). Many students think everything they read is important. They therefore assume that *everything* must be in their answer.

In working with struggling readers who generally maintain this perspective, I've found that modeling important details using a highlighter or a yellow crayon helps. I also use a pencil to leave tracks in the margins for later reference. Whatever way you choose, all those tracks (highlighted or penciled) are important. They become the keys to the answer kingdom. But, we need to show kids how this process works.

I first explain the purpose of the task, which of course is related to a prompt. For instance, it might be to find reasons for why the *Titanic* sank (use something really interesting when modeling). I begin by reading aloud, then stop here and there to think aloud, highlight, and jot in the margins. When I think something is really important, I put exclamation marks or sunbeams shooting out from it. Obviously, this works best when I use a transparency or interactive projection device and the kids use consumable materials. With nonconsumables, use sticky notes.

Afterward, I go back and explain my reasoning for dubbing much of the information as unimportant. For instance, I might say, "If I am searching for reasons why the *Titanic* sank, it would not seem to matter what color the ship was, or how some people didn't use the rescue boats properly, or the number of children on board. That information may have been important in answering other questions, but it does not seem important when I am searching for *why the ship sank.*"

Uncovering the unimportant is an essential piece of this step, because students need to hear us say the words, "This is not important because . . . " They need validation that indeed there are parts of text that have absolutely nothing to do with the question asked. This is especially crucial for students who've continually experienced timed oral assessments that focus on reading words and nonsense syllables.

You can see why "Leave it in?" or "Leave it out?" will continue to plague many students. So let me also suggest that the two best ways to help struggling students discern important from unimportant ideas are modeling unrehearsed, authentic writing and using mindful scaffolding during individual conferences. I can almost guarantee eventual success using these two instructional avenues.

Treat Their Overflowing Confidence with Care

Students are also prone to over-elaborate and get off the topic as their confidence builds. Those who've had a tough time with writing often gain confidence by using the Better Answer protocol—sometimes so much so that they write everything that comes to mind. And how do we tell a student he or she has included too much when this is the same student who, before the Better Answer protocol, wrote one sentence? How do students learn what is too much and what is not enough? And how do we show our new writing zealots how to stay on topic? Read on.

The problem begins once students learn to develop a detailed answer, because they have trouble staying on the topic. Interestingly, part of the reason that their detailed evidence metamorphoses into a new stage of difficulties is that by the time students work their way through Step 2, their cup of confidence is overflowing—and so is their writing. It's a good news/bad news scenario.

Most students move easily through restating the question and constructing a gist answer, and with regular teacher modeling, they also learn where and how to gather the details to support their answers, lengthening and strengthening their responses. But this may well be the first time some students have performed this way in the written world, and they are proud that they have "filled the page." This bolsters the writer's ego. Working off this somewhat inflated ego, they get carried away and write every single thing that comes to mind. Sometimes novices copy every word in the text! At other times they make several connections to their own self-based experiences, deviating from a mandated focus on textual evidence. From their perspective, more is better. So they write and they write and they write.

This is one of the toughest times for me as their teacher, because they're feeling so good about what they're doing. Some of these kids are learning disabled or have consistently needed support in the realm of reading. They joyously call me over to exclaim, "Wow! Look! I filled the whole page!" I find it difficult to tell them that they must now eliminate some of those precious words. This is not only relevant for struggling students and beginning writers; this is a problem for all writers. We hate to eliminate our words—our "little darlings," Stephen King calls them (2000, 222). But even he says we must do this "even when it breaks your egocentric little scribbler's heart." King follows a "Rewrite Formula" a reviewer once gave him: "2nd Draft = 1st Draft − 10%" (2000, 222). Somehow it's comforting just to know that even published authors like Stephen King also have trouble staying on the topic.

First off, kids need to understand that revision usually means cutting, substituting, and (infrequently) extending. But mostly it means cutting. To enter such an elimination of words with grace and finesse, I model . . . and model . . . and model, hoping that what students observe will be contagious. Alas, it usually isn't. However, the modeling still serves as the ground into which I can help them plant their own seeds. In other words, as I chat with them about their writing, I can anchor them back into my modeled piece and what I did while making an analogy to theirs and what they might want to do. Often I leave my modeled pieces posted for ready reference. However, be forewarned: Students still hate to eliminate any part of their writing. Yet they, like Stephen King, eventually learn that "the effect of judicious cutting is immediate and often amazing" (2000, 222). I just keep inviting them to join the Cole Cutting Club.

Establish an Information Pecking Order

Here's one idea that forces kids to discern important from unimportant information. Ask those whose cups are overflowing to number every detail in its order of importance, from most important to least important. This forces some pieces of information into last place, and therefore, into a less important category. We then might suggest that they keep only the essential details, the ones with the lowest numbers, and eliminate those assigned the highest numbers. Sometimes, that's all it takes to focus rambling minds.

Model Unscripted and Authentic TAWAs (Think-Alouds and Write-Alouds)

I might also remind you that Chapter 6 offers a vignette demonstrating a TAWA that focuses on gathering important details. Because these TAWAs are unrehearsed—authentic—students can observe the way in which we struggle to find only the most pertinent facts to present. Showing kids how we think leads them to mimicking the process.

WHEN WRITERS DON'T STICK TO THE TOPIC

Straying off the topic is a common problem for novices—especially when told they must fill up the space offered to them. So they fill it up with whatever comes to mind. That's why "Write more!" doesn't work. Instead, try the following.

Assess for On-Topic or Off-Topic Writing

This activity begins as many of the others, with a brief, curriculum-correlated article, essay, or story that is read aloud to the students, but this time they have a copy of the text to follow along. Afterward, a question related to that piece is displayed where it can be seen throughout the rest of the lesson.

Students each have two large cards: one on which they have written ON-TOPIC in large letters and the other on which they have written OFF-TOPIC. From his or her curriculum-related prompt, the teacher has composed a response, one that maintains the topic *most of the time*, but does occasionally stray off course onto something that is not necessarily closely related. The teacher reads a bit of this answer, and then stops to ask, "Off-topic or on-topic?" Every student should then respond by displaying the related card. Each time, after stopping for a show of cards and possibly some discussion, the teacher continues the process, rereading a little to establish coherence.

This activity can be transferred to later lessons, when the students share their independently constructed responses with partners instead of with the teacher. In a game-like fashion, they can respond to their partner's sentences with the related on-topic / off-topic card.

Know When to Say Good-Bye to a Structure

Whether it's the Better Answer protocol or the five-paragraph essay or 6+1 Trait Writing or any other structural approach, you may discover that structure can be too much of a good thing. That is, we learners do need some structure—a model—to get us started, but whatever the structure is, it won't work for every piece of writing.

This is especially true of the five-paragraph essay. It may prove to be a handy tool *at first*. But within a short time, it tends to draw writers toward irrelevant details as they attempt to fill paragraphs. You see, eventually, that form (an introduction, conclusion, and three more paragraphs for the body) does not align with every writing task. Therefore, what was a crutch becomes a debilitating structure.

For example, not long ago when I was visiting with some students, a few of them had good pieces of writing, yet I noticed a paragraph here or there that seemed like a little lost lamb. When I asked students about it, they sheepishly told me that they were trying to build another paragraph so they'd have five—even though their topic actually needed only an introduction, conclusion, and *two* main points. Consequently, sticking with the structure drew them away from what would have been a sound response.

That's why I suggest we need to eventually ease up on the structures, encourage some leeway, and see what happens. *This is especially important in self-based writing.*

Order Facts to Determine Relevance

When students judge the level of relevance of each piece of selected information, they must come to grips with the fact that some pieces of information are definitely more important than others. And, to make this even more meaningful, responders can be asked to defend their leveled placement for each piece of information (a new twist on the previous suggestion to have students number their details in order of importance).

It's helpful—at least the first few times you do this—to take the reading and selection process off the students' shoulders with a read-aloud that has all the important information already underlined. After reading, display the prompt and ask students to order each piece of underlined information, relating the relevance of each to the prompt. They can actually cut each strip of information apart and decide where it belongs, pasting it into a list of most important to least important details. Having students work together encourages those with differing opinions to critically defend their stances. This is exactly what we're hoping for—students articulating why one fact is more important than another.

After partners finish the task, a whole-group meeting will add another interesting dimension to the issue of most important/least important. However, what we anticipate is that students will come to understand that within each story, article, or essay we read, there is some information that will stand head and shoulders above the rest to support a particular answer.

Sometimes, I write the important details on sentence strips, which can then be moved into a different order as we talk about them in a whole-class situation. Being able to move writing around is very helpful to some students who tend to follow the motto "Once it's down, it's down!" It relieves us of some of writing's permanence and actually encourages revision.

WHEN WRITERS COMPOSE A SHALLOW RESPONSE

Elaborate Using the Better Questions Menu

When a response is shallow but has correct information, we can point responders to the Better Questions Menu. More questions?! you exclaim. Yes, those interrogatives can guide students' thinking toward overlooked channels—and move them a little further than that common five-finger *who-what-where-when-why* tactic. For example, if a student is constructing a self-based response related to his or her favorite holiday, the menu would be a reminder to tell not only *who* was there, *when* and *where* it occurred, but also *how* he or she felt, *what could have* happened, *how it should* be celebrated, and so forth. Regular use of the Questions Menu will imbed its framework in memory, making it a ready resource.

Elaborate Using Definitions

Elaborating using definitions can be useful, especially in the content areas. Plus, it's an easy scaffold. I simply suggest responders insert *which* or *that* after key terms or concepts. For example, if a response mentions *the water cycle*, they might define it in this manner: "The water cycle, *which is the movement of water above and on the earth*, supports life on our planet." And I remind students: "A comma precedes (sets off) *which*, but not *that*."

Elaborate Using Description

Describing and defining are close cousins. And a definition can actually be part of a description. Take the previous example of the water cycle, for instance.

If we were asked to describe the water cycle, we could certainly begin with its definition. And description also incorporates the use of *which* and *that*, as well as interrogatives, each of which leads novices into elaborated phrasing.

For instance, consider the following elaborated phrasing examples related to prompts using *Little House on the Prairie* by Laura Ingalls Wilder ([1935] 2004):

- Laura, *who was Mary's younger sister*, had many responsibilities.
- The family took the windy road *that led to the best place to cross the river.*
- Laura liked the creek, *where the water-bugs skated, the frogs plopped, and the wood-pigeons called.*
- Pa fiddled in the evening *when the moon rose and the firelight danced.*

Once these phrase terms are brought to their attention, students start finding examples of them in the books they're reading. Thus, we know it's internalized.

I demonstrated how phrases can be used to describe, but so can sentences and paragraphs. I spend the major amount of instruction on phrase descriptions, though, because I find that younger students lose their way or get carried away when trying to implement sentence and paragraph descriptions. They may have developed a cohesive piece, but then when they try to tuck in too much description, they and the reader get pulled off-track. So why not keep it simple? Focus on phrases.

Elaborate Using Explanations

Explanation is usually a needed scaffold for young writers who tend to offer only a few basic facts in a response that's supposed to be rich and informative—one that has a page or two of space waiting to be filled. In our explanations, we lean heavily on *how* or *why*, but we infrequently explain *when, where,* or *who.* Yet, the latter three are still a consideration and should be introduced.

Usually, what makes a student's response shallow is the lack of detailed explanation. For example, when writing about fun at an amusement park, many novices might merely mention specific rides without explaining the detailed fun each has to offer. Their writing resembles a list of basic, rather than robust, facts.

There is a time and place, however, for shallow, list-like details—for example, when presented with a small space in which to write. Responders must learn to match space allotments with intention, deciding, "Do I need only the basic details, or do I need a rich, robust response?"

The Petition Framework (see Figure 2 on page 27 and the CD) will help. It suggests using a T-chart to organize explanations. Writers list the basic facts in the left column and the details that elaborate on each basic fact in the right

Other Charts and Visuals

column. For the amusement park response, we might put what was fun in the left column and why it was fun in the right. For example, if we list roller coaster and snack bar in the left column, the chart might resemble this one:

roller coaster	goes high
	stops on top sometimes
	chair swings
	everyone screams
	hang on for life
	music
snack bar	cotton candy mustaches
	snow cones
	smells yummy
	expensive

Once students have logged such details onto their T-charts, it's easier for them to organize, number, and then elaborate this information into sentences explaining why the amusement park was fun. Writers who have experience using graphic organizers know them to be a handy resource, especially for expository writing.

Elaborate Using Examples

Examples can be elicited from a text (for a text-based response) or they can be self-based. Examples are one of the easiest ways to elaborate in self-based writing, yet students infrequently use this strategy. *For example*, in the previous amusement park response, many students will tell what was at the amusement park, but they will not give an example related to what fun looks like, feels like, sounds like, or tastes like. Again, they mention a list that might include the snack bar, the rides, the water-park, and such, but omit examples of what happened to make each thing fun.

What I often do is read aloud over a student's shoulder, stopping midstream to ask, "For example?" or "For instance?" The student's natural inclination is to respond orally, at which point I encourage, "Write it. Write it."

Elaboration through examples is one of the best ways to enrich a piece. Examples tend to add more voice in self-based writing and more details and quoted information to text-based responses.

Examples work well when we are evaluating a person, place, thing, or action. For instance, students often write about people in their families. When they write, "My mom is really nice to me," over their shoulder, I respond, "For example? What's something she did that's nice?"

"She knew I wanted a new pair of wheelies, so last week when we were going—" the student might answer.

"Write it! Write it!" I say. But then I reread to give the writer a head start: "My mom is really nice to me. For example, last week . . . ," leaving the student to finish with the words he or she spoke.

Or when I take papers home and respond to them, I use the margins to nudge, "For example?" Just an ounce of direction.

Examples work well in text-based responses too. When the question asks about a person or an action, the responder can return to the text to use the author's own words to provide an example. Tests sometimes ask, "What kind of a man was da Vinci [or Washington or Shakespeare]?" The student can begin with a basic fact, a gist answer, but then a text example works well with quotation marks to verify that it is a direct quote, all of which makes the responder look good and sound smart.

I also find it helpful to gather a few suitable responses from state websites, project them onto a screen, and ask the students if they see a place where that student could have used the phrases *for example* or *for instance* to elaborate and enrich the response. In this way we help rewrite anonymous Web samples, sculpting them into better pieces.

Elaborate Using Pictures

In classroom writing and projects, embellishment using pictures or photos often works to enhance. However, for assessment purposes, pictures are not usually allowed. Nevertheless, students can still sketch and write captions to help elaborate. Or they might follow the earlier suggestion that used a picture grid. Many of our students feel more comfortable describing, explaining, and telling through pictures, so why not suggest they do just that if it helps them over writer's block?

WHEN CONTENT IS DISORGANIZED

Cut and Paste to Reorder

When I get frustrated trying to organize a piece of my writing, I reach for my scissors. By cutting apart pieces of text, I can more easily manipulate as I consider and reconsider various orders. Sometimes this tactic offers a whole new perspective on a piece, and the writer realizes important facts were omitted.

That's why I always encourage use of this tactic in the classroom. Sometimes I get the feeling that teachers think scissors and paste are things of the past or just for little kids. Not so. They can be handy tools in reorganizing—even for professional authors. (I used scissors twice for this second edition.)

Try Some Transitions

When a response is disorganized chronologically, using time-related transitions can help lead responders to reorganizing. I tell them to try some transitions on and see how they fit. I might suggest *first, next, then, afterward*, and *finally*. As novices attempt to place these properly, they sometimes realize their writing needs to be reordered. (See the transition lists on the CD.)

Better Answer
Transitions Charts

Read the Response Aloud

One of the fastest ways to help responders notice a response is disorganized is by having them read it aloud to someone else. For one thing, it's actually difficult to read a disorganized piece, because it doesn't flow. This becomes evident as the responder reads and listens to his or her own reading. No doubt the peer who's listening will also indicate where the response has gone awry. (See also the activity "In Search of Thick and Thin," page 30.)

WHEN RESPONDERS OMIT CONCLUDING STATEMENTS

Use Color

It's very common for responders to omit concluding statements. That's because they've already answered the question, so the piece feels finished. Using color—green for the introduction, blue for the body of details, and red for the conclusion—as described in Chapter 4, emphasizes the three sections of a response and imbeds this in the minds of the students. I like to respond to a student who's forgotten the conclusion by handing him or her a red pencil or pen, or I put an empty red rectangle at the end—a memorable reminder.

Use a Checklist

When we first start using a checklist, I don't ask the students themselves to mark their own. Instead, I ask their partners to read each item on the list, after which the authors read or show their partners that they have indeed satisfied that item and therefore deserve a check. It is then the partner who marks the list. Afterward, both sign their names at the bottom.

Eventually, I ask the authors themselves to mark their own checklists. As I mentioned earlier, a checklist is not only a reminder, but also a testimonial—one that is tough for most kids to intentionally sabotage. Plus, I've found them to work way better than my own nagging.

WHEN WRITING LACKS FLOW AND COHESIVENESS

See the previous section "When Content Is Disorganized."

Writing that doesn't flow or lacks cohesion is usually disorganized or it needs transitions. In either case, I think you'll find my prior suggestions under "When Content Is Disorganized" helpful.

WHEN STUDENTS GROW BORED

Invite the Students to Develop the Test

After kids have been immersed in prompt-and-response activities, they have a grand time constructing class assessments. Obviously, if everyone is constructing prompts and responses, not all of these can be used. Yet the students won't know which the teacher will select. Of course those who do have their prompts (accompanied by correct answers) selected are proud of their triumph. And if partners work together on this, more is learned and the products are even better. Besides, you'll have worked yourself right out of the job of test developer.

Get Real!

Students rarely get bored with real-world activities. It's all those workbook pages and dittos that bore them. So keep experiences as close to real life as possible—especially after introductory lessons. The world is full of real prompts calling for real responses, from letters to the editor to book reviews to writing for environmental causes.

The CD's Resource section with its live links holds more ideas in this vein, but I'd start by checking the "Letters to the Editor" column in your local newspaper, because often your town's issues are directly related to its youth. After sharing some samples, students themselves get excited about writing a letter to

Web Resources

the editor offering their own two cents on a particular issue. But don't forget to include the boundaries (e.g., maximum number of words) for this task, which are generally printed somewhere in the paper.

When my hometown of Port Townsend, Washington, lost its ferry, fourth graders here wrote to the governor and to the local editor relaying their fact-backed opinions and suggestions. And they received responses—even one from the governor. Kids are never bored when response issues impact their own lives.

Share the Pen

After demonstrating a few think-aloud and write-aloud lessons, partner students and then present dyads with a fairly easy extended-response prompt. Ask them to take turns playing the teacher. That is, one partner begins thinking aloud demonstrating as the teacher did—through writing, while the other partner listens. After a sentence or two, the listening partner shares the pen to have a turn at playing the teacher. Both partners must listen carefully to the other; if they don't, they will have trouble when it's their turn to share the pen.

WHEN WRITERS LACK A SENSE OF AUDIENCE

Explain Why Register Matters

When we construct responses to suit a particular audience, the register of the writing changes. *Register* is the type of language we use within particular social situations or groups of people. We change our register to accommodate our audience. Even young children do this. But in school, students understand their writing usually has one audience—the teacher.

We want students to realize that appropriate register is a vital element in all communication. I explain that it's register that causes *text* messages and *test* messages to each evoke a different kind of response. Even kindergartners can understand that the way they speak to family members is often inappropriate when speaking to their mom's employer, or even their teacher. Some call it respect. Others say it's about being polite. In the end, it all boils down to register.

In the case of prompts, it involves the expectations of those who issue a prompt. When an employer asks, "Why isn't our strategy working?" we would assume that employer expects a vital explanation—whether the prompt was issued by word of mouth or in print form. So let's first make certain kids understand the audience for every piece of writing they compose—and, please, let's not always have the teacher be the one and only audience.

Dramatize, Playing the Stranger

We writers usually write for others—but who are they? If students are asked about the purpose of their writing, research indicates that most say they are writing for their teachers. So even though a prompt may petition students to "Write a letter to . . . " someone other than their teacher, kids see it as a class-room task, so their teacher becomes their audience.

Writers think from a different place when they write for strangers than when they write for their teachers or people they know. When we write for strangers, our writing sounds smarter. However, if the teacher *is* the corrector, how can we move kids beyond that teacher-as-audience perspective? Try these ideas.

After you've played the Stranger with students (as described in Chapter 5), partner students to dramatize playing the Stranger. Ask dyads to draw straws to see who will take the part of a stranger (a visitor from the media is a good one to suggest) to inquire about their partner's response. After a few of these experiences, students begin to realize that responses that sound smart can stand alone without their prompt. Students love this activity and it's even worth all the noise it creates!

Offer a Variety of Audience Experiences

Anytime a writer plans to write in a particular genre for a specific audience, that writer must be thoroughly steeped, like a teabag, in that genre to replicate a similar flavor and quality. For example, if I plan to submit an article to *The Reading Teacher*, I first steep myself in past articles.

Even when articles relate to the same topic, they can sound very dissimilar, for each needs to suit a specific audience in its style, tone, form, and content. For example, articles I've written for *Education Week* have a less sophisticated tone, a softer form and style, and minimal academic content compared with those I've published in *The Reading Teacher*. These two publications have dif-ferent audiences. Basically, we authors must match our style, tone, form, and content to each genre and its audience.

The main way we can help kids slip into an audience-match is by offering them past writing from that same venue. This means that if the audience is state test correctors, then your students should read previous response samples written for that same audience. Similarly, if students are writing for a real-world purpose, such as letters to the editor, they need to read and analyze many published letters to the editor before composing one of their own. Everyone needs a model to mimic sometimes.

Beware though. Know that states that test expository writing do not always march to the same drummer. For example, some states expect a pure form of expository writing, one that with each drumbeat succinctly and cogently pres-

ents substantive factual information (thus residing on the factual end of the Boundaries Scale). In other states, we swing to the music of voice as it adds humor, personal reflections, and opinion to expository responses (thus residing on the creative side of the Boundaries Scale). Are your state expository correctors rewarding those who march to a structured drumbeat or those who swing with the music of voice?

Most published authors will tell you that even they steep themselves before writing. Yet, this remains a crucial, but overlooked, strategy.

What does *your* state assessment audience want? Check the exemplars on your state's website and see.

Pretend!

Kids love to pretend. And they enjoy it not only because it involves pretending, but also because we begin with one of Jon Scieszka's other-side-of-the-story books, such as *The True Story of the Three Little Pigs!* (1996). Once you are able to reference Scieszka's book, read a completely different story with multiple characters and invite the group into a Jon Scieszka perspective. That is, after offering a common prompt, divide the class into the number of characters in the story, and ask each group's members to respond individually to the common prompt from their specific character's perspective.

Once they finish writing, we partner for sharing. Then I ask, "Which of you had a partner whose response you'd like the entire class to hear?" (Notice we are asking students to nominate their partner's response, not their own.) I take those recommendations, read their partner's writing aloud to the class, and celebrate the process.

WHEN STUDENTS HAVE TROUBLE WITH THE CONVENTIONS OF LANGUAGE

Frank Smith tells us, "Conventions do not determine what an author writes. Intentions determine what an author wishes to say, and conventions permit it to be said. Conventions offer the means of expressing an intention" (1982, 92).

Make Sure Kids Know What Mechanics and Conventions Are and Why They Matter

The Oxford Guide to Writing suggests that "*Mechanics* refers to the appearance of words, to how they are spelled or arranged on paper . . . rules gathered under the heading of mechanics attempt to make writing consistent and clear" (Kane 1988, 12). Conventions (including punctuation and spelling) might be thought of as a subcategory of mechanics; however, Kane puts grammar and usage into categories of their own. All are obviously important, for they invite the reader into the content. Without punctuation, spelling, and grammar, content is little more than marks on paper. That is why I group them all under *readableness.*

But I want students to have fully conceived pieces before we get into these cosmetics. That's the way I handle it in my own writing in the real world, as well. Most authors do wait, because conventions don't matter much when a piece is poorly conceived. Nonetheless, it is through the window of conventions that we are able to discern the content.

Under the conventions heading, I include everything that relates to the overt readableness of a piece. Indeed, this is no small consideration. There are tons of books devoted to the teaching of conventions. Entire volumes have been written about grammar alone. But, to address the issue of the readableness of any given piece, I again begin with simplicity and reality.

Spiff Up Your Handwriting

By the time we investigate handwriting, the content is looking good and the kids are sounding smart. Most students are now ready to focus on the response's readableness, that is, conventions, grammar, spelling, punctuation, capitalization—but first and foremost, handwriting. Why handwriting first? Read on.

Extracting handwriting as an entity unto itself on the Better Answer Rubric tells students that we think handwriting is pretty important. Both handwriting and conventions concern the cosmetics and mechanics of the piece. We might enter the handwriting conversation by asking, "If the reader cannot easily read what has been written, how might that affect the assessment?" Apparently, those who write and assess the National Assessment of Educational Progress (NAEP) agree, because they warn students right up front: "When you write your response, be sure your handwriting is clear." This caution arrives even *before* "Think carefully about each question" (National Center for Education Statistics 2007).

I like the way Peter Elbow sculpts this issue. He says, "When the glass is fogged up, we look at the glass. The glass is all we see. As soon as it gets unfogged we ignore it and see through it to the scene outside" (1981, 94). This is a good metaphor to share with kids, because they need to know why it is important to write neatly, and why they must place a priority on bringing the conventions to an optimal level.

Interestingly, we discover that our students are better handwriters than we might have believed, as becomes evident each time I introduce the Better Answer Rubric to a group of kids. Handwriting improves overnight. No kidding!

So the influence of the scale alone will help. But here are a few strategies that worked for me.

Handwriting Strategy #1: First Impressions Count

To me, it seems logical to begin with the issue of readability as it relates to handwriting and neatness. "Why do I believe handwriting and neatness are so important?" you might ask.

My response: "Because if your handwriting is a mess or your paper is smudged, the reader is inclined to feel that the content is probably a mess too." To impress handwriting's importance, I share the following true story with students. There's no better way to explain the poignancy of literary cosmetics than by revealing the impact of sloppy handwriting on the real world.

I explain to students that on employment applications and important tests, those who have neat paperwork with legible handwriting are more apt to come out on top. As a matter of fact, a teacher in our district had a number of students write exactly the same answer, but she told half of them to write using sloppy handwriting, and the others she asked to write very neatly. She then gave the papers to teachers throughout the school to correct. Invariably, the neat papers received better scores even though, except for the quality of handwriting, the answers were exactly the same. When I tell the kids this true story, I also tell them that this is not mean or evil. It's life. Sad, but true: People judge on appearances. I like to be up front with kids, because they appreciate that kind of honesty. However, I also make certain they understand that it is not so much the shape of each alphabet letter, but more a matter of spacing words and letters and keeping the quantity of erasures limited. In other words, neatness matters.

The mere act of beginning by indenting, a somewhat mindless habit that can be easily instilled, makes a student look smart. Most teachers tend to have students use a two-finger indenting width before they begin writing. When kids indent—especially struggling students—I celebrate, "Wow! You're lookin' smart with that wide-space indenting!"

I place a similar importance on keeping to evenly placed beginnings for each line on the page. These are easy to accomplish, but can have a major effect on the overall result. Furthermore, these strategies help students feel like they have control over their products.

Handwriting Strategy #2: Share the Pen

Here's a sure way to do two things at once: (1) show the responder what neatness looks like (including how to erase) and (2) motivate that student to reach for the next rung on the neatness ladder.

We begin with a responder's completed rough draft, which he or she is preparing to copy over. I suggest, "Let's share the pen. I'll copy over the first sentence and you can copy over the next one." I don't remain there for the entire effort, but just that initial impetus is usually enough to get the neatness vibes up and running. My examples sit there calling for other neat sentences. (This is also a great technique for novices who tire during the copying-over period, because it relieves them of part of the "work.")

In the end, the final product will appear neater and the student will be scaffolded forward by the mere fact that your writing is right next to his or hers. Plus, the individual attention gives kids confidence.

Handwriting Strategy #3: Make the Commitment

The first time I introduce the Better Answer Rubric to a class, I explain, "Every time you do a brief, extended, or essay response in any subject, we will be attaching this rubric to your work so that you can keep track of your progress in developing an answer." I then suggest that they circle the area that will be their focus for that particular task that day. "Each time we use this rubric," I explain, "I would like you to focus on one part in particular, so that on any given paper your circled area will most likely end up being an area where you show improvement. Choose any of the six this first time, but pick one in which you truly believe you will be able to show a quality performance and, hopefully, receive a 3."

Most all students choose the same area as their first focus. Can you guess which one? Yes, it's handwriting. You see, 95 percent of them know that they have some control over their handwriting, even though they do not always use that control. Nor, for that matter, do we ourselves always use it. However, adults do spiff up handwriting when it counts—when it's important to look good. And we need to confess this to our students.

Once they circle "Writes very neatly" as their focus, looking for an optimal score in that area, they often get it. The second area for their choice of focus is usually "Restates question in the answer," because it, too, is one over which they quickly have considerable command. Thus, in a very short time, they're able to receive a top score in two areas—even the struggling students! This makes everyone feel good and look smart.

When papers do obtain a quality appearance, I make sure that I draw that to the students' attention, and I usually try to connect it to the real world. I hold up Joe's paper and say, "Wow! If Joe handed this in as a job application and I were his boss, I would really look at him in a positive way. See how neat his paper is? That predicts for me that the rest of his work will also be neat and well done. And, he even indented! That really makes you look smart!" These are very easy ways for students to look good, which then gives them the impetus to sound smart.

I suggest that the most important aspect of conventions is the overt appearance of the piece, that is, what the eye sees even before it attempts to decode the content. I speak here of spacing and smudges, legibility, and sharpened pencils. What will the reader's preconceived notion be—even before he or she actually begins to read the piece?

Conventions—Don't Give Up Hope

Here we are at a place where teachers often display their most negative predictions: "There is no way you are going to get Maria to spell correctly!" or "Say what you want, Natasha Smith will never learn where periods belong!"

I must say that when I began working with that group of struggling fifth graders, I, too, thought, "Whatever I do, I cannot see how I will ever get them to use acceptable conventions!" I had tried for a year to get Joey to use periods, but he still did not use them! And I figured he probably never would. However, I was wrong. Very wrong.

My explanation for how that group of students moved over the conventions hump is this: When they first began to use the Better Answer protocol, they wrote very little—just two or three sentences. They wore their defeatist attitudes like a gray veil, and this affected everything they did. Once they understood how to restate and answer the question, however, their attitudes began to change and the veil lifted. Their confidence grew. And, by the time they were filling the page with details, it seemed to me that they had also begun to see themselves in a new light. I truly believe that they decided that if they could do all that, they were not going to allow conventions to hold them back.

Their final products therefore often had near-perfect conventions, especially compared with the initial pieces they had produced. I was taken aback as much as you will be. With that said, let's move on to some additional strategies to help students improve conventions in their writing.

When Writers Have Trouble with Spelling

This is a tough one! How can a student who cannot spell do well on an assessment that involves spelling? A seeming conundrum?

One thing is sure: There are certain times, even for adults, when spelling will be a problem if we cannot use a dictionary or spell-checker. However, there are a few strategies that appear to help a struggling speller. We adults use these strategies, too, because we all become struggling spellers at times. Therefore, the following should sound familiar.

Spelling Strategy #1: Write It Five Ways

The first spelling strategy that I teach students when they are editing their essay's conventions is to write the questionable word in a number of ways on another piece of paper. "When the correct spelling pops out at you, use it," I say. "However, if you are still in doubt, do what we adults do," which is the second strategy I teach.

Spelling Strategy #2: Use a Synonym

The second strategy is this: If in doubt, use a synonym. Why take the chance of having a word marked wrong if there is a suitable synonym? I tell the students, "If I have to jot a quick note to the principal or to a parent, and I'm not sure of the spelling of a word and have no time to look it up, you better believe I use a synonym!" The same thing happens often when an employee must write something to her superior. People in doubt who don't have a spell-check use a synonym.

A couple of mini-lessons are all students need to internalize this strategy. I sometimes think they especially like it because it seems like the teacher is suggesting they cheat! But I explain that it's not cheating—it's a real-life way to solve a spelling problem.

One last point regards spelling words in informal writing or rough drafts, that is, writing in journals or taking notes. It's important that students understand the difference between the risks we take on drafts and the risks we do not take on tests that score our spelling. In the real world, if we are being evaluated on a particular behavior, most adults are wise enough to monitor their risk-taking. Why shouldn't we teach kids to do the same thing?

Spelling Strategy #3: Use What's Right There

Another obvious strategy that is sometimes overlooked involves using the prompt itself and other text information to spell words correctly. This means that no restatement should be misspelled, because the words are right there in the question. I tend to have a fit if students misspell words that are right there in print.

The real problem presents itself when the students must listen and respond without text, which does not happen quite so frequently; at least in school, it doesn't. However, some state assessments do have a listen-and-respond section. In this case, there are still words in the prompt that can be accessed for spelling reference. And, quite often, proper nouns with multiple spellings, such as names, will be right there in the prompt. However, for other unknown spellings, the preceding two strategies often solve the problem.

Spelling Strategy #4: Use a High-Frequency Word List

The last and most time-consuming spelling strategy concerns teaching students the high-frequency words that they are likely going to need. The Rebecca Sitton spelling program, based on the most commonly used words in student writing, is very helpful as an instructional sequence for struggling spellers. When students learn how to spell the words they use most frequently in their writing, it can have a dramatic influence.

Consider this: If students learn to spell the first twenty-five words on the Sitton list, research demonstrates that they'll spell 33 percent of their writing correctly; when they learn the first 100 words, they'll have 68 percent correct. Focusing on the mastery of at least the first 100 or so words helps even the most challenged spellers to reach a higher level of competence.

The Rebecca Sitton website can provide more information, including the research: http://sittonspelling.com.

WHEN WRITERS DISREGARD PUNCTUATION

Edit at the Ends of Lines

I remember when my own children would bring home their school compositions upon which the teacher had strategically corrected all their errors. However, the only times they noticed the teacher's corrections were when I drew their attention to them or when they had to copy their work over, and even then it was a mindless endeavor. In other words, they were not actually learning anything and would probably make the same errors again. In fact, they did.

So what can we teachers do when time or the number of our students limit us from having individual conferences and we must take students' papers home to mark them? First and foremost, *do not mark the exact error*. Instead, place error marks at the ends of lines, rather than above or on an error. (This works to improve grammar and spelling edits too.) Here's how it works.

For the students who are better at conventions, I merely put a check mark; if there are two errors, I put two check marks at the end of the line. For struggling students, I place a more revealing mark, such as "sp." for spelling, or "p." for punctuation. Regardless, students must identify the specific errors themselves and edit accordingly.

When we mark at the ends of lines, the students themselves must investigate where the errors lie and repair them. In the process of each search, they are learning.

The first time I use end-marks and return the papers to the students, it is helpful and less time-consuming to have them partner, so they can collaboratively find and edit errors. After they understand the operation, they can undertake the task independently. Because the emphasis here appears to be on errors, I must add that each paper also contains an equitable quantity of positive remarks.

When Writers Get Discouraged

Compare Past Performance Using Progress Portfolios

A quick way to remotivate students toward more readable writing is to have them compare their present piece with previous pieces. Just ask them to go to their progress portfolios and lay out their papers in order of neatness. Students who steadily improve (which is most of them) deserve a celebration—a high five! You might also give them a moment or two to share that progress with a friend. Often, that's all it takes to get them headed down the writer's path to better answers.

Celebrate Small Improvements

Jennifer Allen (2008) offers a wonderful celebration idea on the Choice Literacy website: http://www.choiceliteracy.com/public/606.cfm. She suggests that, instead of *teachers* using sticky notes to celebrate the attributes of a student's writing, the *kids* sticky-note their classmates' writing with positive remarks. What's more (and I love this part), we leave those sticky notes on our students' writing and then post both the writing and the accolades so that the public can read the walls of celebration. And one last point: We make certain everyone is represented.

It never ceases to amaze me how a kind word here or there can work wonders. The media often portrays us teachers as people who correct and look for errors; but to me, teaching is about looking for the good stuff—and nothing is too small to be celebrated. Although this area is important enough to deserve thirty pages, suffice it to say that the mere act of holding a teaching certificate connotes a level of kindness and caring. We need to put that kindness out in front—always.

Why not invite the kids into the kindness circle, as well? Take five minutes now and then to ask students to trade papers with someone. That partner's task is to find every good thing he or she can about the partner's response. They can jot these brief compliments on sticky notes, placing each atop the response. I model the process first and call it "Lookin' for the good stuff."

And wouldn't it be great if this perspective carried over into other facets of life as well? Famous authors and artists tell of teachers they had who saw the good stuff in them when they could not see it in themselves. Furthermore, neuroscience now has evidence indicating that, for both the giver and the receiver, compassion salves the neural pathways for learning. It's a win-win interaction!

Classroom Vignette

Demonstrating Assessment in Action

I've spent considerable time offering background and methods related to assessment and our response to it. Now let's see what it looks like, sounds like, and feels like.

This vignette takes place during a one-on-one conference, a time when the teacher has an opportunity both to celebrate a student's response and to scaffold him forward in one area. Notice how this teacher affirms Antonio's use of a conventions strategy, but leaves him with a new strategy that will support his area of need.

Ms. Powers pulls Antonio's written response to yesterday's social studies task from the pile on her desk. She glances at the attached Better Answer Rubric scores as she invites Antonio to meet with her at the table on one side of the room. As teacher and student sit down beside each other, Ms. Powers smiles and compliments, "Antonio! You did much better this time on your social studies written response task. Look at this." She slides the paper in front of his eager eyes.

Before Antonio has a chance to dwell on his mistakes, the teacher points to the positive areas of his paper and comments, "I was really pleased to see that both the restatement and the gist answer were perfect! I loved your top bun in the response.

"And, look at this! You scored a 3 in conventions this time! Only one tiny spelling error. Did you use any strategies that enabled you to do such a fine job on spelling this time?" Ms. Powers asks.

"I made sure I went back to the book spelling. You said we could use our books to spell, so I double-checked everything," Antonio responds somewhat proudly.

"Well, it sure paid off!" the teacher adds. Then she goes on to another aspect of the response.

"We can both see an area needing improvement too," Ms. Powers reminds.

"Yeah, the details. I had trouble with those," the student confesses.

Ms. Powers thinks carefully about how she wants to address this issue so as not to evoke a defeatist attitude in Antonio, yet still develop a sound strategy for improvement. "Antonio, the thing I notice about your details is that, although you found three really good details, you did not explain them. You just kind of dropped them, as is, into the answer so that now they sound lost and lonely. They need an explanation to back them up. Let me read them to you."

The teacher reads aloud Antonio's answer. "The Mississippi River became an important body of water in the United States because it provided this country with a great natural resource. Its water has been used for travel, shipping, and power. That is why it is an important body of water.

"Antonio, in your answer I found out that the Mississippi is an important body of water because it is used for travel, shipping, and power, but what do you think I am wondering about that travel or shipping or power?" the teacher asks.

"I don't know. Maybe like where they travel . . . or maybe what gets shipped," Antonio responds.

"Sure! And we talked all about those things. I knew you knew that. And right now, I noticed you're using question words to help you explain more—like telling *where* they travel, and *what* gets shipped. You can easily make your answer far richer and more informative by using those techniques. So next time, when you reread your answer, please look for your details and see if you have explained—if you've elaborated on them enough so that some stranger would know what you meant. Okay?" Ms. Powers asks.

"Okay," Antonio answers with a shy smile.

"So, Antonio, what will you do next time you write a response?" the teacher asks, encouraging a commitment statement from the student.

"I'm gonna look at my details and see if I told enough so that the Stranger would know what I mean," he responds.

"And what technique could you use?"

"Our question words," Antonio immediately responds.

"Great! I can't wait to read your next response. It's gonna be even better than this one! Tap Sam on the shoulder as you pass his desk, please. I need him next," Ms. Powers requests as she reaches for another paper from the pile, and Antonio leaves the table.

WILL THIS PROTOCOL WORK IN EVERY CLASSROOM?

The Better Answer protocol is much like any other process we teach or are taught. If it is implemented daily across the curriculum, it will have a major impact on student performance. And districts across this country tell me that it has. However, if it is mentioned briefly here and there, the effects will be far less notable.

Therefore, I suggest you use this protocol often. The students love it because it empowers them. Teachers tell me again and again that it builds confidence—probably the major missing ingredient in those who perform poorly in school, on the job, or anywhere.

However, the Better Answer protocol is only the beginning. It is the mere framework upon which students will build deeper, richer responses rooted in multiple genres from a variety of subjects. Eventually, we'll barely be able to see that framework undergirding their exquisite and captivating responses.

CHAPTER 10

AFTERWORD: GET REAL

*Written language is for stories to be read, books to be published,
poems to be recited, plays to be enacted, songs to be sung,
newspapers to be circulated, letters to be mailed, jokes to be told,
notes to be passed, cards to be sent, cartons to be labeled, instructions to be followed, designs to be made, recipes to be cooked, messages to be exchanged,
programs to be organized, excursions to be planned, catalogs to be compared,
entertainment guides to be consulted, memos to be distributed,
announcements to be posted, bills to be collected, posters to be displayed,
cribs to be hidden, and diaries to be concealed.
Written language is not for having your ignorance exposed,
your sensitivity bruised, or your ability assessed.*

—Frank Smith, *Joining the Literacy Club: Further Essays into Education*

As the first edition of this book took shape, I pondered whether I really wanted to write it. Although I was confident it would help students construct test responses, it bothered me that it did not unfold much beyond an initial structure or protocol. Yet, I'd worked with enough teachers to know that they would not let the buck stop with my book's last chapter. *Better Answers* would offer them the initial steps, a valid and developmental entry into the process. But once students internalize that basic structure and are able to construct acceptable responses, most teachers move beyond the bare bones of this fundamental protocol. When they do, each teacher's "afterword" unfolds in ways that move beyond the test and on into interesting and relevant real-world responses. That is, they and their students get real.

Accordingly, mindful teachers immerse their students in the reading and discussion of real-world articles, enticing them with interesting and relevant issues—ones that often call for a written response. Their students compare essays' grand variety of forms and afterward emulate the standards of those authors they've read. To support their journey, I've included on the CD a bibliography of resources (for both print resources and websites in live-link form). Please use this raft of sources to help your students get real and to turn your students on to exciting reasons to write.

If you want kids to develop more mature, self-based essays and responses, nurture them away from the protocol's focus on assessment applications, and instead, use brief and interesting articles and essays by authors the students recognize. You'll ignite curiosity and interest with essays penned by people like Steve Young, Shaquille O'Neal, Jim Brown, Jack Kemp, and Bill Cosby, all of whom have published in *Chicken Soup for the Soul* (Canfield and Hansen 1993) and other books in that series. I witnessed eighth-grade struggling readers actually head for the mall after school to buy *Chicken Soup for the Sports Fan's Soul* (Canfield et al. 2000) after I had used a few poignant essays during class. There are now tons of Chicken Soup books with essays that correlate well with our curricular intentions. For instance, they include authors such as Helen Keller, Roald Dahl, Gloria Steinem, Theodore Roosevelt, Ralph Waldo Emerson, Rudyard Kipling, and Viktor E. Frankl. These texts demonstrate the real reasons that people write self-based essays—they write to celebrate people, their deeds, their triumphs, and their challenges.

Use sources listed on this book's CD to tantalize your students with authentic essays by young people just like them—kids who have found their voices and their causes and who have published their essays on websites such as www.connect2earth.com and in paperbacks such as *Teen Ink* (which is also a magazine) and *Taste Berries for Teens*. Many of these articles are relevant and meaningful to younger students as well as teens.

Some teachers will take this a step further by encouraging their own students to contribute to some of these ongoing publications. They show them what reviewers have said in their online reviews. They lead students to examine numerous reviews and critiques for patterns worth emulating. Then, they demonstrate how to go online and publish a critical review of a CD or book on the Barnes and Noble or Amazon website. Yes, teachers who understand what writing is all about invite their students to construct essays and letters for real-world purposes, to publish their work, to be committed to causes, to be heard. The scaffolding into these more complex texts will occur with grace and finesse if each step forward includes articles and essays that maintain a high level of student interest.

To get real using text-based writing, introduce your students to sites dedicated to curricular issues in science, social studies, and technology—sites whose publications examine climate change, the plight of the poor, struggles for autonomy, the influence of new technology, advances in health care, and alternative fuels. Use your curriculum as a guide—one that leads right into the real world. Show students how real-world text-based writers construct articles and responses, and then invite your students into the act.

So please, move beyond a test curriculum. Offer your students real essay writers to emulate. Offer them real issues to question. Offer them real causes for which they feel compelled to write responses. Offer your kids a tool through which they can help change the world. Offer them authentic reasons to write. For indeed, this is what response writing is all about. It's not about tests in school.

Essay writing is about citizens who care enough to pick up the pen and write. Their authentic response says, this is who I am, and this is why I feel this way; this is what I know, and I think you should know it too.

Just as the Better Answer protocol is a basic structure, a first step into response writing, so should answers constructed on performance assessments be but a first step. When kids are immersed in a curriculum of rich and real essay and response writing, they will approach today's detached, standardized assessments reveling in the confidence that can be created only by reading and writing for real purposes. Indeed, they will know how to look good and sound smart, not only on tests, but also in real life.

Give your students the gift of authentic text—texts that correlate with your curriculum, but remain richer and far more exciting than textbooks and, most obviously, workbooks; authentic writing written by "real" people grappling with "real" issues; texts that coax kids to turn on and tune in.

APPENDIXES

The documents in the appendixes are organized in the same way as they're presented on the CD. Some of these documents are in the appendix in full-page size. Others are presented in smaller versions, with multiple documents on one page. These smaller documents will give you a quick visual reference, but to use them in your classroom, you'll want to print these documents from the CD. Please note that the lesson plans, PowerPoint slides, and sample student responses that are on the CD are not all included in these appendixes; only a sample of each is offered here.

LESSON PLANS AND POWERPOINT SLIDES

A

Sample Lesson Plan

LESSON I.1

TOPIC: Prompts Are Everywhere: Text-Based and Self-Based

SCAFFOLDING LEVEL: Modeling/demonstration and guided participation

GOAL: Students will observe as the teacher demonstrates, and then students will participate in analyzing and collecting a variety of self-based and text-based prompts.

MATERIALS:

- Projection device
- PowerPoint slides for Understanding the Prompt

- Variety of self-based and text-based samples from state websites and living (real-world) prompts (see live links in the CD's Resources folder)
- File folder labeled "Collected Prompts"
- Chart paper
- Markers

PROCEDURE:

Part 1: Explain what a prompt is and where prompts are found, offering a variety of school and living prompts. Invite students to share some prompts they've heard or read.

Part 2: Use the PowerPoint slides for Understanding the Prompt to discuss the difference between a self-based and a text-based prompt. Then, show students a variety of prompts and ask partners to decide which are text-based and which are self-based. Share partner results in a whole-class discussion. (Be sure to also include both kinds of prompts from your own state's past assessments.)

CLOSURE:

Part 3: Ask students to collect prompts throughout the next few days—both living and school prompts—so the class can develop a running list. Each student should add his or her example to the list during free time.

Sample PowerPoint Slides

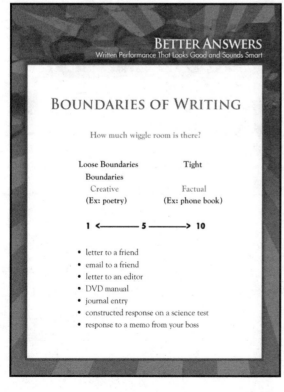

Sample Student Responses

THE CITY MOUSE AND
THE COUNTRY MOUSE (RESPONSES)

PROMPT: Why did the Country Mouse decide to go back home? Be sure to include details from the story in your answer.

> Because it was too danger in the city. And that not his kind of home. He like the country Because it paeceful He like corn and root. I like the part when the country mouse go home Because the city is not his Kind of home, I think the country should live in the country. And the city mouse should live in the city

> The Country Mouse was tramandtsly scared. The Country mouse said: " You live in danger." The Cnitery maue and the City Mouse ate corn and something else.

> The country mouse said this is not a good place, because it is very loud sound and in the country it is not no sound the two mouse got out of the couner the door open and the two mouse got up and the country mouse said the country is quiet and I am going to the country because it is quiet.

CHARTS AND VISUALS

Better Answer Sandwich Charts

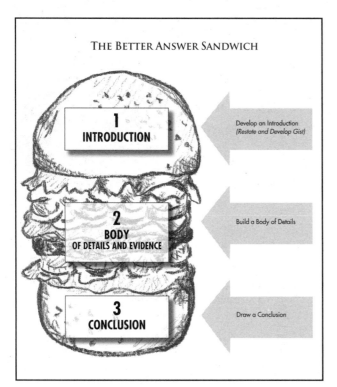

THE BETTER ANSWER SANDWICH

1 INTRODUCTION — Develop an Introduction *(Restate and Develop Gist)*

2 BODY OF DETAILS AND EVIDENCE — Build a Body of Details

3 CONCLUSION — Draw a Conclusion

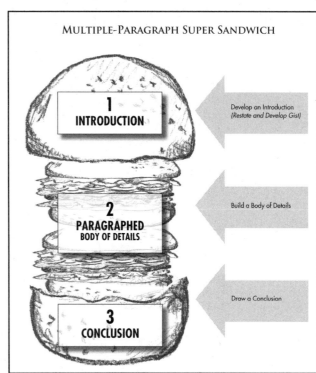

MULTIPLE-PARAGRAPH SUPER SANDWICH

1 INTRODUCTION — Develop an Introduction *(Restate and Develop Gist)*

2 PARAGRAPHED BODY OF DETAILS — Build a Body of Details

3 CONCLUSION — Draw a Conclusion

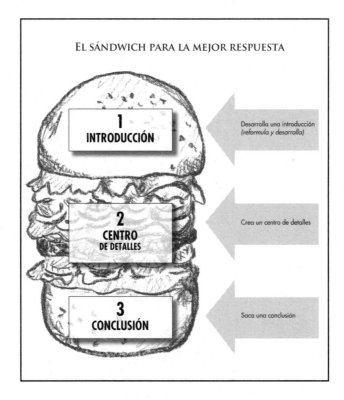

EL SÁNDWICH PARA LA MEJOR RESPUESTA

1 INTRODUCCIÓN — Desarrolla una introducción *(reformula y desarrolla)*

2 CENTRO DE DETALLES — Crea un centro de detalles

3 CONCLUSIÓN — Saca una conclusión

Better Answer Transitions Charts

RESTATEMENT TRANSITIONS

- Little Red Riding Hood was not afraid of the wolf because . . .
- The wolf ran to Grandmother's house to . . .
- Father got rid of the wolf by . . .
- Little Red Riding Hood was afraid when . . .
- Little Red Riding Hood would not have been bothered by the wolf if . . .
- Little Red Riding Hood did not leave for Grandmother's house until . . .

TRANSITIONS FOR EVERY PURPOSE

Transitions That Order

Chronological Order

first	finally	next
at last	second	near the bottom
at the top	the following	to begin with
afterward	then	heretofore
additionally		

Order of Importance

most/least important	most/least significant
most serious	major/minor factor

Order of Effect or Relatedness

as a result	related to this
on the other hand	in connection
related to this	unrelated to this

Transitions That Demonstrate

Transitions That Show Cause

because	as a result
for this reason	so
therefore	consequently

Transitions That Show Contrast

however	whereas	on the other hand
while	but	moreover
yet	despite this	

Transitions That Show Comparison

similarly	and
like	again
in like manner	much the same as
also	furthermore
likewise	

Transitions That Show Examples

for instance	to illustrate
for example	that is

THE TRANSITIONS SANDWICH

Use Transitions to Sound Smart!

Transition gist using
In the following,
Here are/is, To explain

Transition evidence pieces using
First,
Most/Least important, To begin, Most serious,
Most/Least significant,
At the top, A major/minor factor,
In the beginning,
Next,
Then, Essentially, However, Whereas,
Although, Nevertheless, Even so, On the other
hand, Related to this, Unrelated to this,
Near the bottom

Transition conclusion using
That is how/why/when/where/who . . .
Finally, In the end,
To summarize

Better Answer Organizers

THE BETTER ANSWER ORGANIZER

The Better Answer Organizer

1. Introduction
   Restatement ·············►

   General/gist answer ·······►

2. Details for evidence ·······►

3. Concluding statement ·······►

↑
Reread

GOLDILOCKS AND THE THREE BEARS BETTER ANSWER ORGANIZER

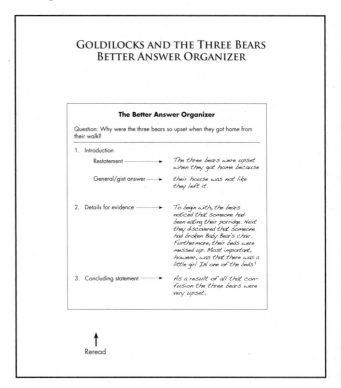

The Better Answer Organizer

Question: Why were the three bears so upset when they got home from their walk?

1. Introduction
   Restatement ·············► *The three bears were upset when they got home because*

   General/gist answer ·······► *their house was not like they left it.*

2. Details for evidence ·······► *To begin with, the bears noticed that someone had been eating their porridge. Next they discovered that someone had broken Baby Bear's chair. Furthermore, their beds were messed up. Most important, however, was that there was a little girl IN one of the beds!*

3. Concluding statement ·······► *As a result of all that confusion the three bears were very upset.*

↑
Reread

LITTLE RED RIDING HOOD BETTER ANSWER ORGANIZER

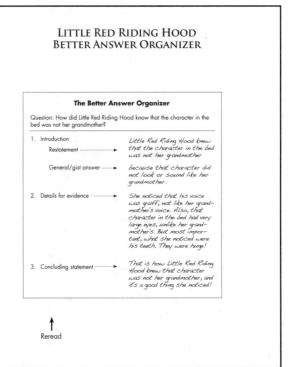

The Better Answer Organizer

Question: How did Little Red Riding Hood know that the character in the bed was not her grandmother?

1. Introduction
   Restatement ·············► *Little Red Riding Hood knew that the character in the bed was not her grandmother*

   General/gist answer ·······► *because that character did not look or sound like her grandmother.*

2. Details for evidence ·······► *She noticed that his voice was gruff, not like her grandmother's voice. Also, that character in the bed had very large eyes, unlike her grandmother's. But most important, what she noticed were his teeth. They were huge!*

3. Concluding statement ·······► *That is how Little Red Riding Hood knew that character was not her grandmother, and it's a good thing she noticed!*

↑
Reread

Other Charts and Visuals

PETITION FRAMEWORK

Key Petition Terms	Meaning	Framework	Examples
Analyze (common with why and how)	Separate into its parts.	An ordered list framework containing parts or steps	Analyze the personality of the main character.
Compare	Examine, noting similarities and differences.	Venn diagram to show differences of each with likeness in the center	Compare two ways of doing something.
Contrast	Examine, noting the differences only.	T-chart (two columns below a heading) to contrast left to right	Contrast two or more approaches.
Define	State a precise meaning or the basic qualities of something.	An ordered list or outline framework	Define the term used.
Discuss (common with why and how)	Present background information with supporting or descriptive details.	T-chart with important factors on left, details on right	Discuss the minor events leading to a major event.
Describe (common with why and how)	Convey an idea, qualities, or background information.	Semantic web: subject in middle, surrounded by numbered qualities	Describe a person, place, thing, or event.
Evaluate	Place judgment, but support using details.	T-chart listing pros next to cons	Evaluate the actions, behaviors, or decisions of individuals or groups.
Explain (common with how and why)	Make clear or offer reason.	T-chart listing facts and supportive details	Explain an action or how/why something happened.
Give/provide	Offer facts related to topic.	T-chart using facts and supportive details	Give several reasons, examples, possibilities, alternatives.
Review	Examine major elements again, sometimes using a critical perspective.	Outline or list framework	Review paths followed, steps taken, important events.
Tell (common with how and why)	Offer facts related to topic.	T-chart using facts and supportive details	Give several reasons, examples, possibilities, alternatives.
Use	Do the task in a specific manner.	Outline or list framework	Use details or information to support.
Write	Usually use as a prompt for a specific task.	Outline or list framework	Write: about; telling; explaining; describing.

BETTER QUESTIONS MENU

Who is . . .
Who was . . .
Who can . . .
Who does . . .
Who did . . .
Who will . . .
Who might . . .
Who should . . .
Who could . . .
When is . . .
When was . . .
When can . . .
When does . . .
When did . . .
When will . . .
When might . . .
When should . . .
When could . . .
Where is . . .
Where was . . .
Where can . . .
Where does . . .
Where did . . .
Where will . . .
Where might . . .
Where should . . .
Where could . . .
How is . . .
How was . . .
How can . . .
How does . . .
How did . . .

How will . . .
How might . . .
How should . . .
How could . . .
What is . . .
What was . . .
What can . . .
What does . . .
What did . . .
What will . . .
What might . . .
What should . . .
What could . . .
What if . . .
Why is . . .
Why was . . .
Why can . . .
Why does . . .
Why did . . .
Why will . . .
Why might . . .
Why should . . .
Why could . . .
Which is . . .
Which was . . .
Which can . . .
Which does . . .
Which did . . .
Which will . . .
Which might . . .
Which should . . .
Which could . . .

QUANTITATIVE GISTS

Clues to the Answer: Closed Restatements with a Quantitative Gist

- There are several reasons for this.
- I can offer a number of reasons for this.
- Here are four ideas that support my perspective.
- Let me explain all of the reasons for this.
- There are five contributing circumstances.
- I'll discuss each problem in the following.
- A number of details/facts verify this.
- Here are some of the reasons why.
- Many things contribute to this problem.

QUESTION CONNECTIONS

	Time: Past Present	Prediction	Character	Setting	Events	Problem-Solution	Cause-Effect	Time Order	Compare Contrast	Description	Evaluation
Who is											
Who was											
Who can											
Who does											
Who did											
Who will											
Who might											
Who should											
Who could											
Who had											
Where is											
Where was											
Where can											
Where does											
Where did											
Where will											
Where might											
Where should											
Where could											
Where had											
When is											
When was											
When can											
When does											
When did											
When will											
When might											
When should											
When could											
When had											
Why is											
Why was											

QUESTION CONNECTIONS (CONTINUED)

	Time: Past Present	Prediction	Character	Setting	Events	Problem-Solution	Cause-Effect	Time Order	Compare Contrast	Description	Evaluation
Why can											
Why does											
Why did											
Why will											
Why might											
Why should											
Why could											
Why had											
What is											
What was											
What can											
What does											
What did											
What will											
What might											
What should											
What could											
What had											
How is											
How was											
How can											
How does											
How did											
How will											
How might											
How should											
How could											
How had											
Which is											
Which was											
Which can											
Which does											
Which did											
Which will											
Which might											
Which should											
Which could											
Which had											

Draw Conclusions That Sound Smart!

Make Connections!

- to *self*
- to *world*
- to *other texts*
- to the *author's craft*

Avoid Pronoun Substitutions

In Text-Based Restating: Avoid Pronoun Substitutions...

...such as:
"She knew he was not her grandmother."

"Bike Trail" Introductions—Good or Bad?

Dear Board Member,
    I agree with the people who are suggesting bike paths for our town. Here's why I feel bike paths would help make our town safer and healthier.

Dear Board Members,
    I like bike paths because they are fun. I have a new bike to ride on bike paths.

Dear Board Members,
    I think the idea of constructing bike trails for bikers is a good one. Let me offer you several sound reasons why I think bike trails would help our community.

Dear Board Member,
    I've read that the town is thinking about making bike paths, and I think this is a good idea. Bike paths help us exercise and stay healthy. They give us someplace safe to ride a bike. Plus, our moms won't have to worry about us so much. Let me explain why I want bike paths for our town.

Dear Board Member,
    Do you ride a bike? I do. That's why I want bike paths for our town. I cannot believe that anyone who rides a bike would not want bike paths. If you do not ride a bike, maybe you don't want bike paths. However, I hope you get a bike soon.

SAMPLE TEXTS, PROMPTS, AND RESPONSES

Text of Tales and Fables with Prompts

THE CITY MOUSE AND THE COUNTRY MOUSE

Retold by Ardith Davis Cole

A City Mouse and a Country Mouse were acquaintances, so the Country Mouse one day invited his friend to come and see him at his home in the fields. The City Mouse walked and walked until he came to the home of the Country Mouse. A little while after City Mouse had arrived, they sat down to a dinner of barleycorns and roots, which tasted very much like the earth from which they came. The food did not appeal to the guest, and before long he broke out with, "My poor, dear friend, you live here no better than the ants in the ground. Now, you should see how I live! My place overflows with a vast variety of wonderful tastes of every sort. You must come and stay with me, and I promise you, you shall live in the lap of luxury."

So, the next day when the City Mouse returned to town he took the Country Mouse with him and showed him a bountiful quantity of flour and oatmeal and figs and honey and dates. "Indeed, how fortunate you are," exclaimed the Country Mouse, for he had never seen anything like it. So he sat right down to enjoy the plentiful meal his friend provided.

But before they had even begun to eat, they heard footsteps, and then the door of the room opened and someone came in. "Hurry," whispered the City Mouse in a frightened voice. "Hide!" The two mice scampered off and hid themselves in a narrow and exceedingly uncomfortable hole in a far corner of the room. They waited for what seemed like hours. Eventually, when all was quiet, they ventured out again. No sooner had they begun to nibble than someone else came down the hall and opened the door. Off they scuttled once more.

All of this was too much for the visitor. "Good-bye," said Country Mouse, "I'm off. You live in the lap of luxury, I can see, but you are surrounded by dangers, whereas at home I can enjoy my simple dinner of roots and corn in peace."

PROMPTS:

- Give reasons why Country Mouse could not live in City Mouse's house. Be sure to use information from the story for your answer.

- Describe how the houses of City Mouse and Country Mouse were different. Then tell which one you'd rather live in and why you prefer that one.

THE GRASSHOPPER AND THE ANTS
Retold by Ardith Davis Cole

"Heave-ho! Heave-ho! Heave-ho!" sang out an army of ants hoisting winter wares upon their wee but mighty shoulders. One after another they marched along, replenishing the cache that would assure their survival over the long, harsh months of ice and snow.

A grasshopper sat alongside their trail, playing casually upon his fiddle. He took little notice of the ants' common mission until an overburdened little fellow tripped over the grasshopper's outstretched appendage and went tumbling head over heels. Finally coming to a stop, he found that his load had landed right in the lap of the resting grasshopper.

"Sorry," apologized Ant.

"Quite all right, my friend," responded Grasshopper. "Where are you and your friends going with all that food? Is there a party I'm missing? Do they need a fiddler?"

"Oh no, sir," answered Ant, finally recovering from his spill. "We are preparing for winter."

"Winter! Winter? Why, winter is months away! There is plenty of time before winter. Why work so hard when you can play? Look at me. I'm having a wonderful time here in the sun with my fiddle," coaxed Grasshopper.

"Yes, but when the cold winds blow, you may be sorry you did not work harder when the sun was shining," reminded Ant. "I apologize that I cannot stand here and talk, but there is work to be done. Good-bye."

"Good-bye, my little friend," Grasshopper called, as he leaned back to take his afternoon nap.

Months passed, and Grasshopper continued to play while the ants continued to work. Then, one day when Grasshopper arose to play his morning tunes, thick frost lay upon the ground and a cold winter wind pierced his shell.

"Guess I'd better gather some goods for winter," he muttered to himself. "Br-r-r-r. It turned cold fast." Thus, he began his search for food. Whether collected, eaten, or rotted, the abundance of summer was now gone.

"What shall I do?" cried Grasshopper. "I will surely die.

"Help! Help!" he called. "Help!"

Inside the warm and well-supplied trunk of a dead tree, the ants heard Grasshopper's frantic pleas. Together they decided that his was a lesson well learned, and they had more than enough for a very foolish friend, who would no doubt be far wiser when the warm winds once again brought abundance for all who were wise enough to claim it.

PROMPTS:

• Why were the ants working so hard in the story?

• Describe what kind of a character Grasshopper is. Use information from the story to support your answer.

THE LION AND THE MOUSE
Retold by Ardith Davis Cole

There was once a fierce and mighty lion who enjoyed catching and tormenting little mice before he ate them. It so happened that as he was walking through the grasslands one day, a little brown mouse scurried by. "BAM!" went the lion's paw, down on the tail of that small, furry creature.

Shaking with fear, the helpless victim squeaked, "Oh, please, kind sir, release me and I will someday return the favor."

"HA!" scoffed the lion. "A wee creature like you help the king of the jungle?" Yet, as the lion sat there listening to his helpless prey beg for his life to be spared, the fierce feline's mood mellowed. He began to consider giving this one mouse his freedom. And so he did.

The sun would set many times before the two of them would meet again. It happened one day as the lion was stalking a small animal on the edge of the great forest. Alas, the fierce beast did not notice the snare that had been set by some hunters, and so he walked directly into it. "SNAP!" went the prison of ropes, capturing the large creature in its grip.

"Help! Help! Help!" roared the mighty beast, caught in the net. Not far away the little mouse heard the lion's call for help, so the tiny creature ran as fast as he could, found the trapped lion, gnawed on the ropes, and freed his friend. As they were about to go their own ways, the mouse turned back and said, "You see, my friend, even those who seem small and insignificant can sometimes help the great and mighty."

PROMPTS:

- The lion was not nice to the mouse, yet the mouse helped the lion. Explain what the mouse did for the lion, and then tell why you think the mouse helped the lion.

- Why did the lion think the mouse would never be able to help him? Use details from the story to support your answer.

LITTLE RED RIDING HOOD
Retold by Ardith Davis Cole

On the edge of a deep, dark woods there lived a woodcutter, his wife, and their young daughter. The little girl loved to frolic in the surrounding forest, which was often quite a bit cooler and more damp than her yard. For that reason her mother made her a beautiful red, hooded cape to keep her warm and dry. The child loved the cloak and wore it daily, regardless of the weather. Consequently, everyone called her Little Red Riding Hood.

One day Little Red Riding Hood's mother said to her, "Grandmother is not feeling well, so I'd like you to take this basket of goodies to her, please. Stay on the path and do not dawdle along the way. I must stay home, for the horse is very ill and needs my attention."

Little Red Riding Hood's grandmother lived at the end of a long forest path. The little girl had made the trip numerous times before, but always with her mother or father. However, she loved the walk and was not one bit frightened, as many other children may have been.

Carefully carrying her basket so as not to spill its contents, she skipped along, singing a merry melody. Suddenly, there appeared before her a large wolf, who at first startled the little girl; however, never having met a wolf before, she relaxed quickly when he offered a kind greeting. "Good morning, little girl. Where might you be going on this beautiful summer day?"

"I'm taking food to Grandmother. She is not feeling well. Mother says that this basket of goodies will pick up her spirits. Where are you going, sir?" the little girl asked in turn.

"Oh, no place really. I'm just enjoying the day. Where does your grandmother live?" the old conniver continued.

"At the end of the path in a little pink cottage," Little Red Riding Hood answered, but then remembered what her mother had told her. "I'd better go along now because Mother said I shouldn't dawdle. Bye," she said as she naively started on her way once more.

"Good-bye, little girl," responded the wolf, ducking back into the bushes and then darting off, intent on reaching Grandmother's house before Little Red Riding Hood. He had plans for that little girl—plans that included dinner.

Unbeknownst to Little Red Riding Hood, the wolf arrived at Grandmother's house considerably before the child. He pulled her grandmother out of bed, tied her up, and locked her in the back shed. Then, he found one of the grandmother's nightgowns and her frilly cap, put them on, and crawled under the bedcovers, which he pulled up so as to reveal only his large, bushy, wolf eyes.

Before long, there was a quiet knock at the door. Knowing it was the child, the wolf tried to mimic the voice of an elderly woman, but responded in a rather gruff, deep falsetto, "Come in."

Little Red Riding Hood thought that her grandmother sounded very ill, so she anxiously opened the door and rushed to her bedside. She began disassembling the basket to show her grandmother all the wonderful items Mother had packed. Eventually, the child looked up right into the wolf's huge black, anxious eyes. Red Riding Hood could not help but gasp, "Grandmother! What big eyes you have!"

"The better to see you with, my dear," answered the wolf in his most grandmotherly voice.

"But . . . but . . . but Grandmother, what big ears you have too," the bewildered child whispered, backing away from those strange ears and fearsome black eyes.

"The better to hear you with, my dear," responded the wolf, this time more excitedly. His impatience took its toll, for the bedcovers slipped down a bit, exposing his nose, mouth, and teeth, large enough to swallow a head in one bite!

"And, Grandmother! What big TEETH you have!" Little Red Riding Hood screamed, now fearing the worst.

"The better to EAT you with," snapped the wolf hungrily as he bounded from the bed and snatched the little girl within the blink of an eye.

"And now, dinner!" he exclaimed, licking his chops.

"Help! Help! Help!" shouted Little Red Riding Hood at the top of her lungs. But, by this time the wolf was charging pell-mell back into the woods with the child securely in tow. She kicked and she punched, but try as she might, the wolf was her superior in strength.

Just then, out of the forest depths came Little Red Riding Hood's father and two other woodsmen. Seeing their axes, the wolf dropped the little girl on the path and took off like an Olympic racer. But, he was not quite fast enough because, as the crafty old animal flew by, one woodcutter managed to remove the wolf's tail.

"Oo-oo-oo!" that old devil cried as he created distance between himself and his pursuers.

Within seconds, the wolf's cries blended with the cries of another. "It's Grandmother!" celebrated Little Red Riding Hood. "She's alive!" And they all ran in the direction of the muffled cries.

Soon, the grateful group was all together again, unharmed. "It's time to put my real grandmother back to bed," announced Little Red Riding Hood, "because I think we've seen the last of that awful old animal. But just in case he needs a reminder—" At that point Little Red Riding Hood hung the wolf's tail, which she had been carrying, on a nail by the cottage door. And there it remains to this very day.

PROMPTS:

- How did the wolf fool Little Red Riding Hood? Use details from the story in your answer.

- Little Red Riding Hood was happy until she walked into her grandmother's house. Explain what made Little Red Riding Hood grow suspicious of the wolf when she arrived at Grandmother's house.

THE THREE LITTLE PIGS
Retold by Ardith Davis Cole

Once upon a time there were three little pigs who lived together with their mother in the home where they were born. From dusk to dawn the brothers played together, until the day came when their mother said to them, "Little pigs, you are not so little anymore. It is time for you to go out into the world and seek your fortunes."

The three were excited about the possibilities before them. "We'll travel the world!" shouted the First Little Pig.

"I'll find a wife!" exclaimed the second pig.

But the third and more sensible pig reminded, "Not so fast. We have to first put a roof over our heads. We must build a home where we will be safe, where we can stay warm when it's cold, and where we can raise a family."

"He's right," grumbled the dejected first pig. "Let's get started so we can investigate the more interesting aspects of life."

So, each pig set forth, intent on the goal of building his own house. The first pig was finished quickly, for he built his house from bales of straw he had purchased from a nearby farmer. The Second Little Pig finished shortly after the first, for he had built his shelter of sticks, most of which he'd gathered from the neighborhood, as well as the woods. Both pigs were proud of their efficient ingenuity and were very pleased that they would soon be able to engage in the more exciting facets of life.

However, the Third Little Pig developed a different plan. He decided to build his house out of bricks. He wanted a house that would last forever, one that would keep him safe from any harm. Bricks would make a mighty fortress, he thought. Unfortunately, this would not be an easy task. Each small brick would have to be shaped and dried. Furthermore, it would take considerable effort and time to lay all of them once they were ready. But, the third pig was determined, and brick by brick his house took shape.

Sometimes his brothers went to watch their industrious sibling work. Pig 3 enjoyed their company, but he did not enjoy their teasing. "Think he'll be done by the time he's old and gray?" joshed Pig 2.

"Nah!" responded Pig 1. "It'll take a lifetime." Then, they'd roll on the ground laughing.

Next, they'd try to dissuade Pig 3's intentions. "Come on, Pig 3," nudged Pig 1, "just use straw to finish it. You're making it difficult when it could be so easy." But, the third pig was adamant and continued on, brick by brick. Eventually, he did finish.

It so happened that one day, not long after Pig 3 had completed his project, Pig 1 had a visitor. The First Little Pig heard a knock on the door, so he glanced out the window to see who it was. "Oh, no!" he gasped. "A wolf!" Trying to put off the seemingly inevitable, Pig 1 asked in a polite voice, "Who's there?"

The wolf also disguised his voice and answered, "It is I, your kind neighbor."

Unable to contain himself, the little pig shouted, "You're not my neighbor! You are a wolf! Go away!"

However, the wolf would not be thwarted, but instead continued, "Little pig, little pig, let me come in."

"Not by the hairs on my chinny-chin-chin," stuttered Pig 1.

"Then I'll huff, and I'll puff, and I'll BLOW your house in!" And, that mean old wolf did exactly as he said he would do. Of course it did not take long to level a straw house.

Fortunately for Pig 1, he had dashed out the back door just in time, and he ran as fast as his little pig legs would carry him to the house of Pig 2. He darted through the front door, bolting it behind him. Pig 2 was startled by Pig 1's behavior, and responded accordingly, "What's going on, for goodness' sake?"

"It-It-It's the wolf," stammered Pig 1, out of breath. "He blew my house down!" The words no sooner left his lips than there came a boisterous pounding at the bolted door.

"Little pigs, little pigs, let me come in!" demanded the wolf.

The two pigs hugged each other, and with trembling voices replied in unison, "Not by the hairs on our chinny-chin-chins."

"Then I'll huff, and I'll puff, and I'll blow your house in!" declared the wolf. The pigs did not wait to see what might happen, but instead dashed out the back door and headed as fast as their pig legs could carry them to the third brother's home.

After the wolf had huffed and puffed and puffed and huffed enough to bring down the stick house, he discovered his predetermined dinner was gone. Thus, his temper was raging when he vowed, "I'll have piggy pie for supper yet. They'll not escape this next time."

Meanwhile, Pig 1 and Pig 2 ran into the arms of their brother, who was stunned, but sympathetic. Out of breath and sobbing, they implored Pig 3 to bolt the door and secure the house, for the wolf was on their trail. Calmly, Pig 3 replied, "Sit down in my nice soft chairs, brothers. I'll take care of this bothersome lout." With that, he picked up a large kettle of water and placed it over the flame in the fireplace.

All too soon, there came a most disruptive banging on the door, followed by, "Little pigs, little pigs, let me come in."

Huddled together, the three pigs sang out at the top of their lungs, "Not by the hairs on our chinny-chin-chins!"

"Then I'll huff and I'll puff and I'll blow your house in!" roared the wolf.

"Oh, no, you won't blow a brick house over, Mr. Wolf! There is no way for you to get into this house except for the chimney—and it is too high," the third pig called deceivingly.

So the wolf huffed and puffed until he was all out of breath, but he just could not move one brick in Pig 3's house. But then, he remembered!

"Ha!" responded the wolf under his breath. "They think I can't get up there. Just watch." With that, the wolf pulled a ladder—a leftover remnant from building the house—over to the far wall, positioned it carefully, and began his journey upward. With a hungry smile on his face, the conniving canine entered the chimney. Down he went, down, down, down . . . right into a large kettle of boiling water. Splash!

"Yow!" he screamed, and flew straight back up the chimney. He skipped the ladder and rolled to the ground, vowing never to approach that family of pigs again. And, the last the pigs saw of the wolf were his soggy footprints heading in the direction of the animal burn clinic.

PROMPTS:

- Why were the houses of Pig 1 and Pig 2 so weak? Be sure to use information from the text in your response.

- The three pigs were brothers, but they had different personalities. Describe the personality of each pig. Tell which one you'd like to have as a friend and why you chose that one.

GOLDILOCKS AND THE THREE BEARS
Retold by Ardith Davis Cole

There was once a little girl whose curls sparkled like gold. For that reason, everyone called her Goldilocks. This adventuresome, energetic child lived with her mother and father near a large, dense forest.

Now, Goldilocks's mother was a fearful sort and was forever cautioning her only child to be careful. She especially worried about the nearby forest, where she was certain all sorts of wild animals lurked, waiting to gobble up her sweet little girl. However, that very same woods appeared inviting to the young child, beckoning her to visit, explore, and play along its paths.

Therefore, one day when her mother was consumed with housework, Goldilocks scampered off to investigate the world outside her yard. Before long, she found herself amidst the birds and branches, the bugs and bushes—an interesting place, indeed. As she scurried along, noticing this and that, her attention was drawn to a small cottage in a clearing.

In that cottage lived three bears: Mama, Papa, and Baby. That same morning, as the bears were waiting for their porridge to cool, Baby Bear began to beg, "Walk? Walk? Walk?" So, Mama and Papa decided to let their breakfasts cool and grant Baby Bear her request.

So it was that when Goldilocks stood on tippy-toes to look in the cottage windows, there was no one to be seen. She next went to the entryway, and when she touched the door to knock, it opened a little. Considering this an invitation, she peeked inside. "Hello," she called out, but received no response.

"Hello-o-o-o!" she sang, this time a bit louder. But, still no one answered. So, she pushed the door ajar and walked into the cottage's cheerful kitchen.

When the little girl spotted the three bowls of porridge on the table, she realized how very hungry she was after her long walk. At first, she just sniffed, taking in the rich warmth of the cereal. But, when she could no longer resist, she tasted of the biggest bowl. "Oh! Too hot!" she cried to no one.

Having learned from Papa Bear's very hot bowl, she immediately noticed the steam rising from Mama Bear's bowl and thus circumvented it. However, the third tiny bowl had no steam, and once she tried it, Goldilocks consumed the entire bowl in just a few minutes.

With the cavity in her belly now filled, the little girl ventured into the next room. There sat three chairs—one very large one, one midsized, and, in the far corner, a cute baby's rocking chair decorated with colorful flowers. Goldilocks decided to test the little one, but became so zealous in her rocking that she soon found herself on the floor with the chair around her in pieces. Disappointed, she tried to reconstruct the pieces—alas, to no avail.

By this time, she was becoming very tired, for the walk had been a long one. Yet, when she noticed the stairs, her adventuresome spirit rekindled her energy and up she went. At the top she found one huge room with three beds. There was an enormous bed that looked so inviting that she tried to pull herself up onto it, but it was far too high. Next she tried the somewhat large bed, which was covered with a beautiful quilt and many plump pillows; however, pull as she might, it too was much too high for her to summit. Then, on the opposite side of the room, she discovered a small cot covered with the most wonderful pink blanket one could ever imagine. As she ran her hand across its inviting softness, she decided to lie down just for a minute or two. Alas, she fell sound asleep.

It was then that the three bears came home from their walk. They took one look at the kitchen table and knew they'd had a visitor. "Who's been eating our porridge?" they all shouted.

"And, Baby's porridge is all gone!" exclaimed Baby Bear.

Father Bear ran into the living room with Mama and Baby at his heels. "Oh, my!" cried Mama Bear.

"Someone's been sitting in my chair," they each shouted, echoing each other.

Then, between her tears, Baby Bear sobbed, "Baby's chair. All gone." She continued to cry, so to console her, Papa Bear picked her up. Then, he hugged her and said in a comforting manner, "It's all right. Papa will fix it. Don't cry."

However, considering how his home had been invaded, her father was growing ever so angry. He hurriedly turned to Mama and suggested, "Let's check upstairs." So, the three bears headed for the bedroom.

They dashed into the large room, anxious to discover what was going on. Papa immediately noticed his bed and gruffly grumped, "Someone's been in my bed."

About the same time, Mama also noticed the disheveled quilt and responded, "Someone's been in my bed too."

Then, a very excited Baby Bear squealed, "Someone in my bed! Here her is!" All the commotion startled Goldilocks, who jumped up, took one look at those three incredulous bears, and ran from the house as fast as she could. She ran and ran and eventually ran right into the arms of her mother and father, who had decided to search the forest when they could not find their little girl.

The family hugged and kissed and kissed and hugged, they were so happy to see one another. Finally, when the excitement of their reunion began to wane, Goldilocks looked at her parents, and grateful to be rescued, vowed, "I will never, ever go into the forest alone again." And, they believed her.

PROMPTS:

• Why was the bears' house a mess when they arrived home from their walk?

• Goldilocks made a mess of the bears' house. Explain what the bears will have to do now to rectify the antics of Goldilocks.

Sample Student Responses

PROMPT: Why did the Country Mouse decide to go back home? Be sure to include details from the story in your answer.

> Because it was too danger in the city. And that not his kind of home. He like the country Because it paeceful He like corn and root. I like the part when the country mouse Go home Because the city is not his kind of home, I think the country should live in the country. And the city mouse should live in the City

> The Country Mouse was tramandsly scared. The Country mouse said: " You live in danger." The Cautery mouse and the City Mouse ate corn and something else.

> The country mouse said this is not a good place, because it is veay loud sound and in the country it is not no sound. the two mouse got out of the courer the door open and the two mouse got up and the country mouse said the country is quiet and I an going to the country because it is quiet.

PROMPT: Why did the little mouse say, "Even those who seem small and insignificant can sometimes help the great and mighty"? Be sure to include details from the story in your answer.

> Mouse said even those who seem small and insignificant can sometimes help the great and mighty because he wanted the lion to know he was just as big as the lion. He set that big lion free and so he was just as him. That is why he said even those who seem small and insignificant can sometimes help the great and mighty.

Lion caut mouse and mouse asked him
to let go so then When lion was
caut mouse helped him too. That is
why he said that.

_____ Mouse said that because he
is not small and he proved it!

Get Real for Animals

Log in to myWWF | Sign up | Help

WWF *for a living planet*

About WWF   How You Can Help   News & Facts   FAQ   search

Home > News & Facts > Education > The Basics > Species > Omnivores > Chimpanzee

The Basics

Species
Carnivores
Herbivores
Omnivores
  Bear (Brown)
  Bear (Polar)
  Chimpanzee
    Human Ways
    Social Animals
  Kiwi
  Whale
  Wolf (Maned)
Remarkable Animals
Habitats
Homework Help

Chimpanzee

Our closest relative

Class: Mammalia (mammal)
Order: *Hominidae* (human-like mammals)
Family: *Pan troglodytes* (chimpanzee)

The chimpanzee is more closely related to humans than any other mammal. It ranks 2nd only to humans in intelligence.

The chimpanzee has another close relative called the bonobo or pygmy chimpanzee.

Both species are found only in tropical Africa, mainly West and Central Africa. However Bonobos are found only in the rainforests of the Democratic Republic of Congo.

Chimpanzees enjoy the lush greenery of thick forests but are also found where the forest meets wooded savannas.

In previous times they once inhabited 25 African countries. Now, they are extinct in 4 and nearing extinction in many others.

Height:
1.5 m (Common Chimp)
0.90 m (Pygmy Chimp)

Further information

WWF Global Species Programme: Chimpanzees

Life Span: 45 years

The ape family

The chimpanzee is the 3rd largest ape after the gorilla and the orangutan. A male stands about 1.5 m tall when upright and weighs about 43 kg. It has a pink to brown face and thick, long, brown-black hair. The face, ears, hands and feet are bare. Like other great apes, chimps do not have tails.

Moving about

Chimpanzees have longer arms than legs. They can move on the ground or through trees. On the ground, they run on all fours, but walk upright with toes turned inwards.

While on all fours, they support the weight of their body on the knuckles of their hands. Chimps are scared of falling from trees and rarely swing by their arms as gibbons and orangutans do.

ORANG-UTAN   GORILLA   CHIMPANZEE

What's on the menu?

Chimpanzees are mainly vegetarians, eating leaves, roots, and fruits like wild figs. But they sometimes eat birds, small rodents, and insects. Termites are a favourite snack!

Wild chimps spend about 7 hours a day looking for food, either up in the trees or on the ground. Crevices and cracks in logs are searched for insects, and nests are robbed for eggs and chicks.

Chimps' teaparty?

Chimps sometimes use tools for eating: they dip a grass stem into a termite nest and lick off the termites that crawl up the stem. Sometimes they use rocks for breaking open tough fruits.

When food is plentiful, a large group of chimps assembles for a feast. Adult males drum on the roots of trees or on the ground and other chimps join in a loud hooting chorus. This noise can be heard a long way off, attracting other chimps.

Chimps seem to get most of their water from the fruit they eat. They rarely drink and when they do, they dip one hand into the water and lick it. They also crush leaves into a 'sponge' squeeze the water into their mouth.

Conservation concern

In West Africa, chimps are now very rare because most of their forest habitat has been chopped down to make room for farming. Although chimps are still quite common in other parts of Africa, in some areas people enjoy eating chimpanzees and many are killed for food.

These days, logging companies are moving into new areas of rainforest to exploit them for timber. Not only does this destroy the chimpanzees' habitat, it also means that more people can hunt them.

WWF is helping to conserve chimpanzees by working with African governments to create national parks where chimpanzees will be safe.

Chimpanzee facts

Each adult chimpanzee builds a new, individual tree nest each night for sleeping.

Bonobos can be distinguished from chimpanzees by their black face and red lips, and a prominent tail tuft which is retained by adults - chimpanzees only have one at the juvenile stage.

A A   🖨 Print Page   ✉ E-Mail Page   Add to del.icio.us   Digg This   Web feeds

Privacy   Share Content   Web Tools   Contact   Feedback   Site Map   Commenting?

design & technology by getunik.com

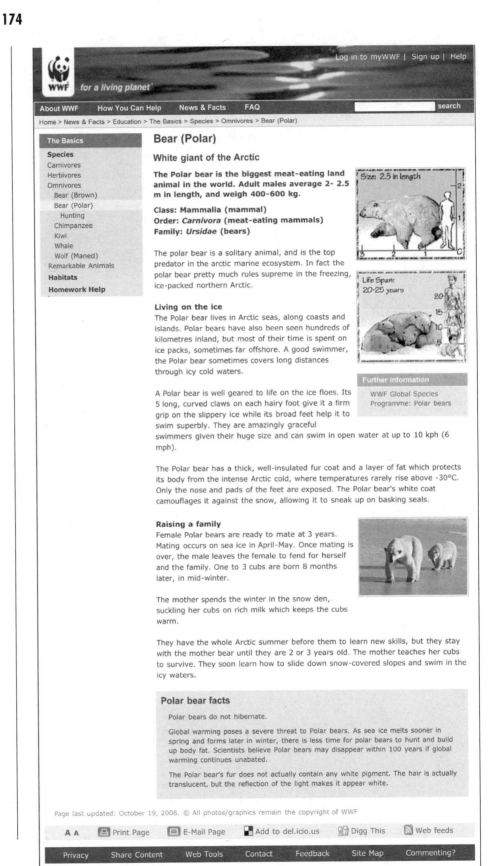

WWF *for a living planet*

About WWF   How You Can Help   News & Facts   FAQ   search

Home > News & Facts > Education > The Basics > Species > Omnivores > Bear (Polar)

The Basics

Species
Carnivores
Herbivores
Omnivores
  Bear (Brown)
  Bear (Polar)
    Hunting
  Chimpanzee
  Kiwi
  Whale
  Wolf (Maned)
Remarkable Animals
Habitats
Homework Help

Bear (Polar)

White giant of the Arctic

The Polar bear is the biggest meat-eating land animal in the world. Adult males average 2- 2.5 m in length, and weigh 400-600 kg.

Class: Mammalia (mammal)
Order: *Carnivora* (meat-eating mammals)
Family: *Ursidae* (bears)

Size: 2.5 in length

The polar bear is a solitary animal, and is the top predator in the arctic marine ecosystem. In fact the polar bear pretty much rules supreme in the freezing, ice-packed northern Arctic.

Life Span: 20-25 years

Living on the ice
The Polar bear lives in Arctic seas, along coasts and islands. Polar bears have also been seen hundreds of kilometres inland, but most of their time is spent on ice packs, sometimes far offshore. A good swimmer, the Polar bear sometimes covers long distances through icy cold waters.

Further information

WWF Global Species Programme: Polar bears

A Polar bear is well geared to life on the ice floes. Its 5 long, curved claws on each hairy foot give it a firm grip on the slippery ice while its broad feet help it to swim superbly. They are amazingly graceful swimmers given their huge size and can swim in open water at up to 10 kph (6 mph).

The Polar bear has a thick, well-insulated fur coat and a layer of fat which protects its body from the intense Arctic cold, where temperatures rarely rise above -30°C. Only the nose and pads of the feet are exposed. The Polar bear's white coat camouflages it against the snow, allowing it to sneak up on basking seals.

Raising a family
Female Polar bears are ready to mate at 3 years. Mating occurs on sea ice in April-May. Once mating is over, the male leaves the female to fend for herself and the family. One to 3 cubs are born 8 months later, in mid-winter.

The mother spends the winter in the snow den, suckling her cubs on rich milk which keeps the cubs warm.

They have the whole Arctic summer before them to learn new skills, but they stay with the mother bear until they are 2 or 3 years old. The mother teaches her cubs to survive. They soon learn how to slide down snow-covered slopes and swim in the icy waters.

Polar bear facts

Polar bears do not hibernate.

Global warming poses a severe threat to Polar bears. As sea ice melts sooner in spring and forms later in winter, there is less time for polar bears to hunt and build up body fat. Scientists believe Polar bears may disappear within 100 years if global warming continues unabated.

The Polar bear's fur does not actually contain any white pigment. The hair is actually translucent, but the reflection of the light makes it appear white.

A A   Print Page   E-Mail Page   Add to del.icio.us   Digg This   Web feeds

Privacy   Share Content   Web Tools   Contact   Feedback   Site Map   Commenting?

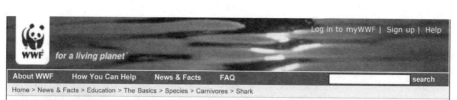

Log in to myWWF | Sign up | Help

About WWF   **How You Can Help**   **News & Facts**   **FAQ**

search

Home > News & Facts > Education > The Basics > Species > Carnivores > Shark

The Basics

Species
Carnivores
  Tiger
  Shark
    Hammerhead Shark
    White Shark
    Tiger Sharks
  Seals
  Penguin
  Timber or Grey Wolf
Herbivores
Omnivores
Remarkable Animals

Habitats

Homework Help

Shark

A WWF-supported ecotourism project centred around swimming with whale sharks (while following strict rules so as not to disturb the animals) has brought a flourishing tourism industry to Donsol, the Philippines.
© WWF-Canon / Jürgen FREUND

Sleek predators of the sea

Many people think that all sharks are ferocious, dangerous animals. This is untrue! There are more than 360 species of sharks, but just 3 kinds of shark (the great white shark, the tiger shark and the bull shark) are involved in most attacks on humans. In fact, a shark is more likely to be killed by a human than the other way around!

Class: *Elasmobranchii* (cartilaginous fish)

The first sharks lived around 400 million years ago, with most sharks developing during the Cretaceous Period (64 million years ago) – the time of the dinosaurs!

Big sharks, small sharks

Sharks vary greatly in size and habit. Whale sharks are the largest of all fish and can grow up to 12 m long and weigh up to 12,000 kg. The smallest sharks are the tiny pygmy sharks which are fully grown at 25 cm long.

Shark food

Sharks are efficient predators. They have a highly developed sense of smell, hearing and sight. They can scent their prey in the water from a great distance. Their sensitive eyes can see clearly even in the dim light of the ocean depths.

Sharks are carnivorous and eat fish, including other sharks. Large species may eat seals, turtles and penguins. Some sharks, like the whale shark and the basking shark feed on plankton. Blue sharks swim in leisurely circles when they are hungry and become increasingly excited when they sense food.

Baby sharks

Most fish lay eggs in the water which are then fertilised by the male. But shark eggs are fertilized inside the female's body. In most species, the eggs hatch inside the female and the babies (called pups) are born alive. Some kinds of sharks, like the catshark do lay eggs, ejecting them in flattened cases known as Mermaid's Purses.

Some sharks that give birth to live babies have as few as 2-3 pups at one time. Others have around 12 and some as many as 70-80. A new born shark is able to swim as soon as it is born and is immediately left to fend for itself by the mother.

Because sharks cannot breed fast like other fish, it means that their numbers can be easily be reduced by too much fishing. This is why scientists believe that shark fishing should be regulated.

Related links

International ban on shark finning adopted

Magnets may save sharks, says WWF

Ray and shark fishing to stop in Mauritanian national park

Whale shark ecotourism contributes to Filipino economy

Problems: Fisheries bycatch

More information

Shark Research Institute

The growing trade in shark fins - often used to make an expensive Asian soup - has become a serious threat to many shark species.

Conservation concerns

Millions of sharks are killed each year by humans. Many are killed deliberately for their fins, which are made into shark's fin soup. This practice is cruel and wasteful, as the fins are cut off and the rest of the shark is thrown back into the sea. Other sharks die in fishing nets set for other fish. Shark meat is popular in many parts of the world. Some species of sharks are now endangered.

WWF is among other conservation organisations leading the fight to save the world's sharks. It is seeking the ban on certain kinds of fishing nets and working to regulate the trade in shark fins.

The growing trade in shark fins often used to make an expensive Asian soup has become a serious threat to many shark species.
© WWF-Canon / Jürgen Freund

Shark facts

Sharks have up to 5 rows of teeth which are replaced as they wear out. A shark can lose up to 30,000 teeth during its lifetime.

Some sharks can swim very fast. The fastest shark is the Mako shark which has been known to reach 32 kph or even faster. It can also leap 6 m above the surface of the water.

Sharks are in every ocean of the world, from icy polar seas to warm tropic waters. Some sharks even swim up rivers.

Sharks have a skeleton made up of a tough, elastic substance called cartilage. They do not have a gas-filled swim-bladder like other fish. Most oceanic sharks must keep swimming forwards to force seawater through their open mouths and over their gills to breathe - otherwise they would suffocate.

A A   Print Page   E-Mail Page   Add to del.icio.us   Digg This   Web feeds

Privacy   Share Content   Web Tools   Contact   Feedback   Site Map   Commenting?

design & technology by getunik.com

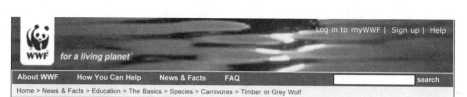

Log in to myWWF | Sign up | Help

for a living planet

| About WWF | How You Can Help | News & Facts | FAQ |

search

Home > News & Facts > Education > The Basics > Species > Carnivores > Timber or Grey Wolf

The Basics

Species
Carnivores
  Tiger
  Shark
  Seals
  Penguin
  Timber or Grey Wolf
Herbivores
Omnivores
Remarkable Animals
Habitats
Homework Help

Timber or Grey Wolf

Dogs' ancestors

Flesh eating mammals (Carnivores)
Class: Mammalia (mammal)
Order: Carnivora (meat-eating mammals)
Family: *Canidae* (dogs)

The wolf is the ancestor of the domestic dog but instead of barking, it howls. Only wolf pups make a high-pitched bark.

There are 2 species of wolf - the timber or grey wolf and the red wolf. The timber wolf has a number of subspecies found in the wilder parts of Europe, northern Asia and India, and North America. Red wolves are very rare and are found in the south-eastern United States. Wolves live in open country and in forests.

The timber wolf is 120 to 200 cm from nose to tip of tail. It is about 70-80 cm tall and weighs between 20 and 60 kg. Timber wolves that live in northern regions tend to be much heavier than those found further south.

Grey wolf (*Canis lupus*).
© WWF-Canon / Chris Martin
BAHR

A timber wolf has strong jaws with sharp canine and carnassial (cheek) teeth for tearing and chewing meat.

Timber wolves vary in colour according to the region they live in. European wolves are grey to greyish brown with some reddish hair on the back. The legs may be paler in colour. On the Arctic coast of Alaska and western Canada, wolves are a mixture of white and grey.

The timber wolf has long, slender legs. It can maintain a steady pace of about 8 kph over long distances.

Hunting in packs
The timber wolf is an intelligent and courageous hunter. Wolves may hunt alone, but usually they hunt in a family pack of 3 to as many as 30 wolves. The pack is led by an 'alpha' male and female, and the rest of the pack is usually made up of their grown-up pups.

Each pack has a hunting territory which they defend from other wolves. Male wolves mark the boundaries of their territories by urinating on bushes or rocks. This behaviour is similar to that of domestic dogs.

Hunting in packs helps wolves kill large animals such as moose or elk. They are good swimmers and when necessary pursue their prey into water.

Timber wolves display remarkable team spirit and cooperation during a hunt. So perfectly is the hunt executed that the pack acts like a single animal.

A big appetite
The timber wolf can eat a lot of meat at one meal and then go without food for a considerable time. Though it does eat large animals like caribou (reindeer), musk oxen, deer and moose, most of its diet consists of of small animals like mice, rabbits and squirrels. It also eats fish, crabs and dead animals (carrion).

Family life
Wolves generally pair for life. Mating takes place in late winter or early spring. Pups are born 2 months later. Before their birth, the she-wolf chooses a den site in a thicket or amongst rocks and lines her den with dead leaves, moss and hair from her belly.

The litter has 4-6 pups. Born blind, their eyes open 5 to 9 days later. The mother wolf takes great care of her young ones, sometimes carrying them in her mouth. They are suckled for 8 weeks, during which time they also eat half-digested food regurgitated (vomited) by the mother and other members of the pack.

The family stays together for some time while the parents teach the pups hunting skills. In about a year, the cubs reach adulthood, but may stay with the pack for longer.

WWF Pandamobile tour 1998-2000 displaying an exhibition about the "Comeback of the Wolf". Michel Terrattaz, WWF animator, explaining to school children where the wolf has been spotted in Switzerland, and which regions/territories are most favorable for its comeback.

© WWF-Canon / WWF Intl. / Abdu Rauf

Conservation concern

The wolf's biggest enemy is man. For many centuries, wolves have been trapped, shot and poisoned because people fear that wolves presented a danger to cattle and sheep. Sometimes they were killed for their fur. Wolves have been virtually exterminated from the continental United States and western Europe, although a few survive in Spain, northern Scandinavia and Italy.

Wolves seldom attack humans, in fact very few records of them doing so exist. As long as there is plenty of natural prey, wolves prefer not to attack domestic livestock.

WWF is exploring ways to strengthen wolf populations in Europe, for example by helping wolves spread into suitable remote areas from areas where they already exist.

Wolf facts

The wolf is the 2nd largest predator in Western Europe after the brown bear.

The territory size of packs of wolves in Alaska and Canada ranges from 500 to 1500 sq km.

A wolf's jaws are so strong it can bite through a moose femur (thigh) in just 6-8 bites.

Page last updated: October 1, 2007. © All photos/graphics remain the copyright of WWF

A A   Print Page   E-Mail Page   Add to del.icio.us   Digg This   Web feeds

Privacy   Share Content   Web Tools   Contact   Feedback   Site Map   Commenting?

design & technology by getunik.com

Home > News & Facts > Education > The Basics > Species > Omnivores > Whale

The Basics

Species
Carnivores
Herbivores
Omnivores
   Bear (Brown)
   Bear (Polar)
   Chimpanzee
   Kiwi
   Whale
     Toothed Whales
     Baleen Whales
   Wolf (Maned)
Remarkable Animals
Habitats
Homework Help

Whale

Giants of the ocean

Whales are part of the cetaceans group, along with dolphins and porpoises. There are over 80 species of cetaceans.

Class: Mammalia (mammal)
Order: *Cetacea* **(Whales, dolphins and porpoises)**
Suborders: *Odontoceti* **(toothed whales)** *Mysticeti* **(baleen whales)**

Further information
WWF Global Species
Programme: Cetaceans

Whales are the giants of the sea. The sight of a great whale swimming in the ocean is unforgettable. Despite being huge animals, whales are not easy to spot because they glide silently along, creating hardly a ripple. They only give themselves away when they come up to breathe and send up gigantic spouts of air and water from their blowholes.

Whales are divided into 2 groups. The baleen or whalebone whales have no teeth, only a flexible horny substance called baleen suspended from the upper jaw, which acts as a sieve or strainer.

The baleen group of whales has 13 species, including most of the enormous whales. Toothed whales, dolphins and porpoises are a diverse group which is made up of more than 70 species and includes sperm whales and killer whales.

The largest mammal
They range in size from the compact minke whale, whose average length is around 8m, to the gargantuan blue whale, which can reach lengths of over 33m and weigh up to 120 tonnes - as much as 32 elephants! Toothed whales are smaller but vary in size, from 1.5m Hector's dolphins to the 18m sperm whale that weighs almost 60 tonnes and is the world's largest carnivore.

Life under water
Whales are mammals which returned to the sea about 50 million years ago and assumed a fish-like form. Their hind limbs disappeared and their front limbs evolved into flippers. Although they breathe air, whales cannot survive on land. Whales that accidentally get stranded on a beach soon die, because the great weight of their bodies crushes their internal organs.

While most whales are ocean-dwelling animals, some toothed whale species live in freshwater.

Whales move their body through the water with the help of their horizontal tail which flaps up and down. Whales can reach astounding speeds. Killer whales can reach 55 kph and some dolphins reach 35 kph. By contrast, humans' top speed does not usually average above 8 kph.

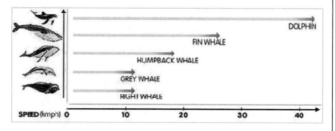

Whales have a thick layer of fat called blubber under their smooth, almost hairless skin which helps them retain their body heat.

There she blows!

Whales can dive deeply and stay down a long time. The Sperm Whale, for instance, can dive down more than 2000m and remain below the surface for almost 2 hours! Like land mammals, whales have lungs and come to the surface of the water to breathe through their nostrils.

A whale's nostrils are called the 'blowhole', situated at the top of the head. A surfacing whale exhales warm air and moisture from its blowhole in a huge fountain. This was mistaken by old-time whalers for a spout of water. You can identify a whale species by the size and shape of its 'blow'! Baleen whales have 2 blowholes whereas toothed whales have just 1.

What do whales eat?

Whales with baleens sieve out plankton, squid and small fish from seawater. Toothed whales prey on a variety of fish and squids. Whales swallow their food whole and have a muscular compartment to their stomach which crushes their food.

The song of the whale

Most whales are social animals and some travel in groups called pods. Whales communicate with each other by singing complex songs made up of a variety of whistles, clicks, low and high-pitched moans, grunts and groans. Some of these sounds are too high or too low-pitched for us to hear, but the noise travels long distances under water. In fact, whale songs are quite beautiful, even to human ears!

Raising young

A Baleen whale baby is born 11 months after mating. Some toothed whales have longer pregnancies. Whales only have one baby at a time and the baby is born tail first and is fully developed. Most whales nurse their young ones for about 6-7 months.

Conservation concern

Whales have been hunted for centuries for their blubber, oils, meat and baleen. Overhunting in the past has brought 7 of the 11 great whale species close to extinction. Even though most commercial whaling stopped 30 years ago, most of these species have not recovered to their original numbers.

The northern right whale shows no recovery at all and is the most endangered large whale with just 300-350 thought to be in existence.

WWF has made saving whales a top priority. It continues to argue against countries which want to resume hunting whales. WWF and other organizations were instrumental in getting the whole of the Southern Ocean and the Indian Ocean declared international whale sanctuaries.

Whale facts

The blue whale's heart is as big as a Volkswagon Beetle!

Small groups of Humpback whales will cooperate to blow 'curtains' of bubbles to herd fish.

Despite their huge size, a number of whales, including the humpback whale, right whales and the fin whale, are able to leap completely out of the water.

A A   Print Page   E-Mail Page   Add to del.icio.us   Digg This   Web feeds

Privacy   Share Content   Web Tools   Contact   Feedback   Site Map   Commenting?

design & technology by getunik.com

Get Real for the Environment

Roadless Forests:
Death by Poison Pill

Conservationists' efforts to protect 58.5 million acres of roadless national forest land suffered a setback in May when the Bush administration announced that it intends to amend this new national policy forest-by-forest. "The administration sugarcoated this news by saying the policy would stand," says Mike Anderson, Senior Resource Analyst in our Seattle office, "but then indicated that Forest Service officials would be allowed to make exceptions based on local conditions. That's another way of saying that the logging industry will have an opportunity to weaken the policy."

The administration explained its action by maintaining that local interests had not been fully consulted in development of the new rules, which bar road building and most logging in these pristine areas. "The truth," says Anderson, "is that there's never been a federal regulation that was based on so much local input." The Forest Service held 600 hearings around the country and reviewed a record 1.6 million public comments.

In addition to pressing its case with the new administration in Washington, the logging industry has gone to court to challenge the policy. Along with seven other groups in the Heritage Forest Campaign, we have won court approval to be involved in these lawsuits in order to present the reasons for moving forward with this policy.

To step up our long-term campaign to help citizens protect our national forests, we have just created a National Forest Activist Training Institute. The heart of it is a series of day-long workshops around the country to share knowledge on how to communicate with the media, conduct research, and mobilize grassroots support, among other subjects.

More than half of the acreage in the national forests has been roaded or otherwise developed, and we believe the one-third of the forest system that is roadless—but currently not protected as wilderness areas—needs to be left just as it is. The benefits of doing so include cleaner air and water, viable habitat for fish and wildlife that need undisturbed areas, recreation opportunities, and the local economic boost that these natural areas provide by luring visitors. The national forests already contain about 400,000 miles of roads, enough to circle the planet 16 times.

You can help defend these roadless areas by urging U.S. Forest Service Chief Dale Bosworth not to amend the rule. (201 14th St., SW, Washington, DC 20090; 202-205-1661)

More information:
www.wilderness.org/roadless.htm

PROMPT: What actions are being taken to protect our national forests? Use the article to support your answer.

PROMPT: Why does this author think road building in the national forests is unnecessary? Support your answer with details from the article.

National Monuments *Under Attack*

Only five months ago conservationists and others were celebrating designation of Upper Missouri River Breaks National Monument as a way to protect a stretch of the river in central Montana. But now there are signs that the Bush administration, U.S. Senator Conrad Burns (R-MT), and Congressman Dennis Rehberg (R-MT) are seeking ways to allow coal-bed methane development and oil and gas drilling there. The resulting rigs, roads, buildings, and traffic would pollute the water, destroy archaeological sites, and damage habitat vital to elk, mule deer, and sage grouse, among others.

The Bush administration has said that it does not plan to undo the 22 national monuments created or expanded over the past five years. (In fact, under the Antiquities Act, only Congress has that power.) "But if they attempt to reduce a monument's acreage and then draw up a management plan allowing those destructive activities that the monument was designed expressly to prevent, it amounts to the same thing," says The Wilderness Society's Dave Albersworth. Across the West, we are working with partners to mobilize public support to block such efforts.

Another threatened monument is Grand Staircase-Escalante in southern Utah. Congressman James Hansen (R-UT), chairman of the House Resources Committee, told the *Deseret News*: "You could easily shrink Grand Staircase. Two-thirds of it is nothing special, just mostly sagebrush." That two-thirds includes the spectacular Kaiparowits Plateau, and its removal from the monument would facilitate massive coal mining. It was that very threat that provided much of the impetus to create this outstanding monument in the first place.

Also facing immediate threats are Ironwood Forest and Sonoran Desert National Monuments, both in southern Arizona. ASARCO, a multinational mining company, has spoken with federal officials about splitting Ironwood Forest into four pieces to accommodate an expanded open-pit copper mine in what is now the heart of the monument. Sonoran may be reduced to permit a power line corridor to slice through the middle of the area and to allow for a car race. Meanwhile, the Bush administration has expressed interest in oil drilling at California's Carrizo Plain National Monument and expansion of commercial fishing at U.S. Virgin Islands Coral Reef National Monument.

"The administration keeps saying that these monuments were established without any effort to hear the views of local residents," says Albersworth. "That's just not true. Interior Secretary Babbitt spent much of last year crisscrossing the West holding public meetings to find out exactly how people felt."

Current Interior Secretary Gale A. Norton and Congressman Hansen have sent letters to governors, members of Congress, and other politicians inviting them to seek changes in the monuments. "These critics like to overstate the quantity of land protected," says Darrell Knuffke, who directs The Wilderness Society's field staff. "The 22 monuments add up to about six million acres. That's just one percent of the land that belongs to all Americans. That does not strike me as an excessive amount of land to leave in its natural condition."

Please contact Interior Secretary Norton (1849 C St., NW, Washington, DC 20240; 202-208-7351) and your representatives in Congress (Washington, DC 20515 for House and 20510 for Senate; 202-224-3121) to urge them to maintain the level of protection these places currently have.

PROMPT: How are our national monuments being threatened? Use evidence from the article to support your answer.

PROMPT: How do those encroaching on national monuments justify their actions? Use evidence from the article to support your answer.

Visit a Place Near You:

| Where We Work |

Search: (Tips)

[ ] (Go)

Bioreserves
Kentucky
Kentucky Home
About the Chapter
Places We Protect
Bioreserves
How You Can Help
Volunteer Opportunities
Events
Slide Shows
Chapter News
Contact Us
Related Links

© Richie Kessler

River Speak

By Richie Kessler

We often talk about how nature speaks to us. Nature may speak to us in many different ways it excites us, calms us, motivates us, wraps us in serenity, or even scares us. It probably speaks to each of us in different ways in this sense, nature is multilingual! I often have wondered if Green River could speak to us, what would it say? And how would we refer to Green River? Is the Green River an it, a he (like old man river), or a she? For now, I believe I will pay it the proper respect and refer to the Green as a "she".

I am sure if she could talk she could tell us how for millennia she has cut through the valley, creating new channels, rediscovering old ones, and making habitats all the time. Similarly, she could describe for us how, as she cut the valley, she also contributed to the formation of the world's largest cave system. Maybe she would tell us of how the most recent period of glaciation, several thousands of years ago, stopped just short of her doorstep, sparing her landscape and topography from eternal alteration and enhancing her potential for the great biological diversity found in her waters even today.

More recently, she might recall how early native Americans fished her waters or sought shelter in her caves. Or how our ancestors shipped supplies down the Green to the Ohio, Mississippi and beyond. She might remember the echo of gunfire as Union and Confederate soldiers battled for positions along its length including sites like Tebb's Bend and Munfordville, or the echo of a Kentucky rifle as a great-great grandfather harvested a squirrel from an overhanging sycamore limb. Maybe she would describe for us how our predecessors used to visit town by crossing her spine on a cable ferry at Greensburg.

She laughingly remembers having her ribs of Brush Creek, Little Barren, Lynn Camp Creek and Russell Creek tickled by the splashing feet of the youth of yesterday. However, she won't hesitate to remind you that, in combination with her tributaries and in spite of efforts to control her, she can become a powerful force worthy of our respect in a matter of minutes. She has caused communities like Greensburg to tremble at her rising waters more than once in history. Her strong pulses have put life into our valleys by richening our soils for agriculture. Her force has powered the production of grist mills like the Montgomery Mill on Pitman Creek and Three Hundred Springs Mill on Green River. Even though she supports and sustains our life, she also is powerful enough to take it away.

As a mother proudly boasts of her children, she would also want us to know that she is home to the greatest fish and mussel diversity of any river system in Kentucky. From Green River dam to Mammoth Cave alone, she is home to 109 types of fishes and nearly 60 different kinds of mussels, many of them exceedingly rare. And you ought to see her basement! Her underground streams contain some of the most unique and rare organisms on earth. Indeed, if she were considered a house and her rooms habitats, she would be one of the freshwater mansions of North America. A Biltmore estate of freshwater diversity! We are fortunate to have so much to care about—so much to conserve.

As impressive as this sounds, however, she might also complain a little. She has earned the right after all. She might relay to us how she has become "stressed out" in recent times as our populations have grown along with our demands on the lands that border her. She would tell us how we have littered her once beautiful cliffs with rubber tires, water heaters, or other modern "throw away" items. Or how we have polluted her waters in a myriad of ways and altered her flow and temperatures. Many of her fishes (~%) and mussels (%) are imperiled, meaning the future is not secure. I guess we could say she is a freshwater mansion in need of some repair. Indeed, nearly seventy miles of her two banks and bottoms are in need of some form of restoration.

Green River would also tell us that she is resilient. Despite the stresses of mankind, upper Green River continues to support an amazing number of fish and wildlife species and a number of human uses. We must remember, throughout its history, this river has sustained itself with or without man (or due to his absence). Alternatively, man has depended on its waters and will continue to do so throughout his existence.

Interestingly, although people have altered the river and threaten it in many ways, it is also people who have the ability to protect the river for future generations. Once, sections of Pitman Creek near Campbellsville were practically devoid of fish life due to pollution by dies and heavy metals from a local industry. When this stress was reduced and, eventually, removed, many species of fishes returned. Through the efforts of many, an underground stream at Horse Cave once regarded as an open sewer now is home to a museum. The site is now a popular tourist attraction where visitors can see aquatic cave life prospering once again. Around 1960 the oil boom in Green, Hart, and Metcalfe counties resulted in petroleum and brine being flushed into many streams. Some of the small streams were virtually killed out. The effects of runoff from Green County were felt all the way to Mammoth Cave. Many of these streams, thankfully, have recovered to some degree.

Even though she is resilient, it is hard to predict the ultimate effect of these cumulative stresses not only on the fish and wildlife but also on the water quality, which affects us all. I interpret her message to be that if given a fair chance she will continue to provide us the various benefits we have come to expect and perhaps have taken for granted, in the past.

Okay, so the Green River doesn't really speak. Maybe she actually depends on us to speak for her. Yes, her people are her voice. But imagine for a minute if she could speak, would anyone listen?

[Back to Bioreserves]

PROMPT: Across the centuries, Green River has changed. Describe two detrimental changes that have occurred and explain what we might do to help Green River recover. Use information from the article in your answer.

PROMPT: Green River is different now from how it used to be. Compare its present state with the way the river was in the past. Be sure to use information from the article to support your comparisons.

ASSESSMENT TOOLS

Better Answer Rubrics and Scales

The Better Answer Rubric

Name_____ Date _____

	Minimally 1	Partially 2	Completely 3
Restates question in the answer	_____	_____	_____
Develops a gist answer	_____	_____	_____
Uses details to support the answer	_____	_____	_____
Draws conclusion	_____	_____	_____
Stays on topic	_____	_____	_____
Writes neatly	_____	_____	_____
Uses proper conventions	_____	_____	_____

The Better Answer Rubric

Name _____ Date _____

	Minimally 1	Partially 2	Completely 3
Restates question in the answer	_____	_____	_____
Develops a gist answer	_____	_____	_____
Uses details to support the answer	_____	_____	_____
Draws conclusion	_____	_____	_____
Stays on topic	_____	_____	_____
Writes neatly	_____	_____	_____
Uses proper conventions	_____	_____	_____

The Better Answer Rubric

Name _____ Date _____

	Minimally 1	Partially 2	Completely 3
Restates question in the answer	_____	_____	_____
Develops a gist answer	_____	_____	_____
Uses details to support the answer	_____	_____	_____
Draws conclusion	_____	_____	_____
Stays on topic	_____	_____	_____
Writes neatly	_____	_____	_____
Uses proper conventions	_____	_____	_____

The Better Answer Rubric

Name _____ Date _____

	Minimally 1	Partially 2	Completely 3
Restates question in the answer	_____	_____	_____
Develops a gist answer	_____	_____	_____
Uses details to support the answer	_____	_____	_____
Draws conclusion	_____	_____	_____
Stays on topic	_____	_____	_____
Writes neatly	_____	_____	_____
Uses proper conventions	_____	_____	_____

The Better Answer Rubric

Name _____ Date _____

	Minimally 1	Partially 2	Completely 3
Restates question in the answer	_____	_____	_____
Develops a gist answer	_____	_____	_____
Uses details to support the answer	_____	_____	_____
Draws conclusion	_____	_____	_____
Stays on topic	_____	_____	_____
Writes neatly	_____	_____	_____
Uses proper conventions	_____	_____	_____

Boundaries Scale

Loose Boundaries   **Tight Boundaries**
Creative   Factual
(Ex: poetry)   *(Ex: phone book)*

1 ◄——————— 5 ————————► 10

Estimate the wiggle room:

- letter to a friend

- email to a friend

- letter to an editor

- DVD manual

- journal entry

- constructed response on a science test

- response to a memo from your boss

Better Answer Checklists

Response Sign-Off Checklist

____ I found all of the petitions and questions in the prompt.
____ I restated all petitions and questions.
____ I constructed a gist in my introduction.
____ I found details to use as evidence.
____ I found ways to insert some smart transitions.
____ I developed a conclusion.
____ I reread my response from beginning to end.
____ I am happy with my response now.

Initials_____ Date_____

Response Sign-Off Checklist

____ I found all of the petitions and questions in the prompt.
____ I restated all petitions and questions.
____ I constructed a gist in my introduction.
____ I found details to use as evidence.
____ I found ways to insert some smart transitions.
____ I developed a conclusion.
____ I reread my response from beginning to end.
____ I am happy with my response now.

Initials _____ Date _____

Response Sign-Off Checklist

____ I found all of the petitions and questions in the prompt.
____ I restated all petitions and questions.
____ I constructed a gist in my introduction.
____ I found details to use as evidence.
____ I found ways to insert some smart transitions.
____ I developed a conclusion.
____ I reread my response from beginning to end.
____ I am happy with my response now.

Initials _____ Date _____

Response Sign-Off Checklist

____ I found all of the petitions and questions in the prompt.
____ I restated all petitions and questions.
____ I constructed a gist in my introduction.
____ I found details to use as evidence.
____ I found ways to insert some smart transitions.
____ I developed a conclusion.
____ I reread my response from beginning to end.
____ I am happy with my response now.

Initials _____ Date _____

Response Sign-Off Checklist

____ I found all of the petitions and questions in the prompt.
____ I restated all petitions and questions.
____ I constructed a gist in my introduction.
____ I found details to use as evidence.
____ I found ways to insert some smart transitions.
____ I developed a conclusion.
____ I reread my response from beginning to end.
____ I am happy with my response now.

Initials _____ Date _____

Response Sign-Off Checklist

____ I found all of the petitions and questions in the prompt.
____ I restated all petitions and questions.
____ I constructed a gist in my introduction.
____ I found details to use as evidence.
____ I found ways to insert some smart transitions.
____ I developed a conclusion.
____ I reread my response from beginning to end.
____ I am happy with my response now.

Initials _____ Date _____

Response Sign-Off Checklist

____ I found all of the petitions and questions in the prompt.
____ I restated all petitions and questions.
____ I constructed a gist in my introduction.
____ I found details to use as evidence.
____ I found ways to insert some smart transitions.
____ I developed a conclusion.
____ I reread my response from beginning to end.
____ I am happy with my response now.

Initials _____ Date _____

Monitoring Spreadsheets

Class Monitoring Spreadsheet

Task or Test _____ Date _____

Students' Names	Room	Answer Content						Answer Readableness		
		Restates	Gist Answer	Details as Evidence	Draws Conclusion	Stays on Topic	*Content Total Score*	Hand-writing	Conventions	*Readableness Total Score*

SAMPLE Class Monitoring Spreadsheet

(before implementation of Better Answers)

Task or Test ___"The City Mouse and the Country Mouse"___   Date _____

Students' Names	Room	Answer Content						Answer Readableness		
		Restates	Gist Answer	Details as Evidence	Draws Conclusion	Stays on Topic	Content Total Score	Hand-writing	Conventions	Readableness Total Score
Andrew	5	1	1	2	1	1	1	2	2	2
Carmelita	5	1	3	2	2	2	2	2	2	2
Mohab	5	1	1	2	1	1	1	1	2	2
Beline	5	1	3	2	3	2	2	2	1	1
Steve	5	0	0	0	0	0	0	0	0	0
Delanie	5	2	2	1	2	2	2	2	2	2
Keoh	5	1	1	1	1	1	1	2	1	1
Amanda	5	1	1	1	2	1	1	3	3	3
Tai	5	3	3	2	2	2	2	2	1	1
Roomel	5	3	3	2	1	1	2	3	2	2
Julia	5	3	3	2	2	2	2	1	1	1
Michael	5	3	3	3	3	3	3	1	2	2
Francis	5	1	2	1	2	2	2	3	2	2
Nutando	5	3	3	3	1	2	3	3	1	2
Shiasta	5	1	1	1	1	1	1	1	1	1
Tiando	5	3	3	2	2	2	2	1	2	2
Mavis	5	1	1	2	1	1	1	2	1	2
Ryad	5	2	2	3	2	2	2	3	2	2
Layla	5	2	2	2	1	2	2	3	2	2

Individual Student Monitoring Spreadsheet

Student Name

Task or Test	Date	Answer Content						Answer Readableness		
		Restates	Gist Answer	Details as Evidence	Draws Conclusion	Stays on Topic	*Content Total Score*	Hand-writing	Conven-tions	*Readableness Total Score*

RESOURCES

Print Resources

BOOK RESOURCES

This section has been developed to provide a raft of background related to locating good essays; however, it seemed important to explain just exactly what essays are before investigating their sources.

Essay writing falls somewhere between creative writing and expository writing, presenting facts and evidence, but doing so in a narrative style. It's inherently nonfiction, yet shaded with interpretations. Essays can be in article or report form, but according to Webster's New World Dictionary (Neufeldt 1991), each must be a complete piece of writing. The tone, although often serious, can also be "relaxed and frequently humorous" (Concise Columbia Encyclopedia 1994, 202). It is that tone that hues the piece with voice, and it is the expectations of the audience that define the tone.

Furthermore, an essay is "expressive of the author's outlook and personality" (Neufeldt 1991, 464), and for that reason, point of view can subtly, as well as flamboyantly, shade the meaning inherent in the writing. There is nowhere that I know of that this can be more readily experienced than on National

Public Radio (NPR), where short essays are read regularly and, depending on the author, reflect this side or that of an issue. NPR listeners seem to enjoy heavy bias, whereas those correcting examination papers may not. Students need to know this. They need to investigate the essay's grand number of forms. This bibliography will provide an entry point for such a journey.

Books with Essays and Articles for Grades 3–8

Allenbaugh, K. 2000. *Chocolate for a Teen's Soul: Life-Changing Stories for Young Women About Growing Wise and Growing Strong.* New York: Simon and Schuster.

Baxter, K. A., and M. A. Kochel. 1999. *Gotcha!* Englewood, CO: Libraries Unlimited.

Canfield, J., ed. 1998. *Chicken Soup for the Kid's Soul.* New York: Scholastic. (Essays are written by kids.)

Canfield, J. Chicken Soup for the Soul Collection. Titles include *Sports Fans, Pets, Dogs, Preteens,* and *Teens.* New York: Scholastic.

Carlson, R. 2000. *Don't Sweat the Small Stuff.* New York: Hyperion.

Cooper, G., and C. Cooper. 2001. *New Virtual Field Trips.* Englewood, CO: Libraries Unlimited. (Contains a gazillion websites with short pieces related to every curricular area.)

Covey, S. 1998. *Seven Habits of Highly Effective Teens.* New York: Fireside.

Drew, B. A. 1997. *100 Most Popular Young Adult Authors: Biographical Sketches.* Englewood, CO: Libraries Unlimited.

Duey, K., and M. Barnes. 2000. *Freaky Facts.* New York: Aladdin.

Editors of Canari Press. *Random Acts of Kindness; More Random Acts of Kindness; Random Acts of Kindness for Kids.* Berkeley, CA: Canari Press.

Haven, K. 1995. *Amazing American Women: 40 Fascinating 5-Minute Reads.* Englewood, CO: Libraries Unlimited.

———. 1998. *Close Encounters with Deadly Dangers: Riveting Reads and Classroom Ideas.* Englewood, CO: Libraries Unlimited.

Haven, K., and D. Clark. 1999. *100 Most Popular Scientists for Young Adults: Biographical Sketches*. Englewood, CO: Libraries Unlimited.

Jaffe, A., ed. 2001. *Heart Warmers of Love*. Holbrook, MA: Adams Media.

LaFontaine, P. 2000. *Companions in Courage*. New York: Warner Books.

Meyer, S. H., and J. Meyer. 2000. *Teen Ink*. Deerfield Beach, FL: Health Communications. (Written by teens.)

McElmeel, S. L. 1998. *100 Most Popular Children's Authors: Biographical Sketches*. Englewood, CO: Libraries Unlimited.

————. 2000. *100 Most Popular Picture Book Authors and Illustrators: Biographical Sketches*. Englewood, CO: Libraries Unlimited.

Mendoza, P. M. 1999. *Extraordinary People in Extraordinary Times: Heroes, Sheroes, and Villains*. Englewood, CO: Libraries Unlimited.

Nelson, P. 1993. *Magic Minutes*. Englewood, CO: Libraries Unlimited.

Portalupi, J., and R. Fletcher. 2001. *Nonfiction Craft Lessons: Teaching Information Writing K–8*. Portland, ME: Stenhouse. (Essays are found in the appendix.)

SARK. *Inspiration Sandwich*. Berkeley, CA: Celestial Arts.

Williams, T. 2001. *Stay Strong: Simple Life Lessons for Teens*. New York: Scholastic.

Wyatt, F. R., et al. 1998. *Popular Nonfiction Authors for Children*. Englewood, CO: Libraries Unlimited.

Series Books with Essays for Grades 3–8

Extraordinary Americans Series
Readability 3–4; J. W. Walch (www.walch.com):
16 Extraordinary American Women
16 Extraordinary Asian Americans
16 Extraordinary Hispanic Americans
16 Extraordinary Native Americans
16 Extraordinary Young Americans

Walch Super Readers
Readability 3–4; J. W. Walch (www.walch.com):
Amazing Rescues
Baffling Disappearances
Creepy Creatures
Daring Escapes
Great Crime Busters
Great Disasters
Mysterious Places
Scary Tales
Stories of the Presidents
Unbelievable Beasts
Unlikely Heroes

MAGAZINE RESOURCES

(Most of these magazines also have a website.)

Byline, P.O. Box 130596, Edmond, OK 73013.

Calliope: Exploring World History, Cobblestone Publishing, Inc., 30 Grove St., Peterborough, NH 03458.

Canada and the World, R/L Taylor Consultants Publishing, P.O. Box 7004, Oakville, ON, Canada L6J6L5.

Child Life, Children's Better Health Institute, P.O. Box 7468, Red Oak, IA 51591.

Children's Digest, Children's Better Health Institute, P.O. Box 7468, Red Oak, IA 51591.

Cicada, Carus Publishing Co., P.O. Box 7705, Red Oak, IA 51591-0705.

Cobblestone, Cobblestone Publishing, Inc., 30 Grove St., Peterborough, NH 03458.

Colorado Kids, The Denver Post, 1560 Broadway, Denver, CO 80202.

Creative Kids, Prufrock Press, P.O. Box 8813, Waco, TX 76714.

Cricket, Cobblestone Publishing, Inc., 30 Grove St., Peterborough, NH 03458.

Current Events, Weekly Reader Corp., P.O. Box 2791, Middletown, CT 06457.

Dolphin Log, The Cousteau Society, 870 Greenbrier Circle, Suite 402, Chesapeake, VA 23320.

Dragonfly, National Science Teachers Association, 1840 Wilson Boulevard, Arlington, VA 22201.

Faces, Cobblestone Publishing, Inc., 30 Grove St., Peterborough, NH 03458.

Footsteps, Cobblestone Publishing, Inc., 30 Grove St., Peterborough, NH 03458.

Hit Parader, 63 Grand Ave. #200, River Edge, NJ 07661.

Hot Dog Magazine, Scholastic, Inc., 555 Broadway, New York, NY 10012.

How on Earth! Vegetarian Education Network, P.O. Box 3347, West Chester, PA 19381.

Junior Scholastic, Scholastic, Inc., 2931 E. McCarty St., P.O. Box 3710, Jefferson City, MO 65102.

Kid Magazine Writers, http://www.kidmagwriters.com.

Kids Discover, P.O. Box 54209, Boulder, CO 80323-4209.

Know Your World Extra, Weekly Reader Corp., 3001 Cindel Dr., Delran, NJ 08370.

Muse, Cobblestone Publishing, Inc., 30 Grove St., Peterborough, NH 03458.

National Geographic Kids, National Geographic, P.O. Box 2330, Washington, DC 20013.

National Geographic World, National Geographic, P.O. Box 2330, Washington, DC 20013.

New Moon Magazine, P.O. Box 3587, Duluth, MN 55803; http://www.new-moon.org.

Odyssey, Cobblestone Publishing, Inc., 30 Grove St., Peterborough, NH 03458.

Owl, Young Naturalist Foundation, 56 The Esplanade, Suite 306, Toronto, Ontario, Canada M5E1A7.

Racing for Kids, Griggs Publishing Co., P.O. Box 500, Concord, NC 28026.

Scholastic Action Magazine, Scholastic, Inc., 2931 E. McCarty St., P.O. Box 3710, Jefferson City, MO 65102.

Scholastic Choices, Scholastic, Inc., 2931 E. McCarty St., P.O. Box 3710, Jefferson City, MO 65102.

Scholastic Math, Scholastic, Inc., 2931 E. McCarty St., P.O. Box 3710, Jefferson City, MO 65102.

Scholastic Search, Scholastic, Inc., 2931 E. McCarty St., P.O. Box 3710, Jefferson City, MO 65102.

Science World, Scholastic, Inc., 2931 E. McCarty St., P.O. Box 3710, Jefferson City, MO 65102.

Skipping Stones: A Multicultural Magazine for Kids, Skipping Stones Magazine, P.O. Box 3939, Eugene, OR 97403.

Spider, Cobblestone Publishing, Inc., 30 Grove St., Peterborough, NH 03458.

Sports Illustrated for Kids, Sports Illustrated, P.O. Box 60001, Tampa, FL 33660-0001.

Teen Times, Future Homemakers of America, Inc., 1910 Association Dr., Reston, VA 22091.

Thrasher (Skateboard) Magazine, High Speed Productions, Inc., 1303 Underwood, P.O. Box 884570, San Francisco, CA 94124.

Time for Kids, Time, Inc., Time & Life Building, 1271 Avenue of the Americas, New York, NY 10020-1393.

U*S* Kids, Carus Publishing, P.O. Box 7468, Red Oak, IA 51591.

Voices of Youth, Communications Publishing Group, Inc., 106 West 11th St., Suite 250, Kansas City, MO 64105.

The Wall Street Journal Classroom Edition, Wall Street Journal, P.O. Box 300, Princeton, NJ 08543.

Weekly Reader: News For Kids, 200 First Stamford Place, P.O. Box 120023, Stamford, CT 06912-0023.

Wild West, 602 South King Street, Suite 300, Leesburg, VA 22075.

Wildlife Conservation, 185th St. & Southern Blvd., Bronx, NY 10460.

Young Voices, Young Voices, P.O. Box 2321, Olympia, WA 98507.

Zillions: The Consumer Reports for Kids, Zillions Department, P.O. Box 51777, Boulder, CO 80321.

Web Resources

LINKS TO ARTICLES, STORIES, PROMPTS, AND MORE

http://andromeda.rutgers.edu/~jlynch/Writing/links.html (Information related to everything about writing, from copyrights to web publishing to grammar.)

www.amazon.com (Amazon website has hundreds of book reviews.)

www.bn.com (Barnes & Noble website has hundreds of book reviews.)

www.cbs.sportsline.com/mlb (Scores, stats, and links to articles for every current sport.)

www.cdc.gov (Resourceful government website with many brief, easy articles related to health, wellness, and safety for grades 5+.)

www.chinaberry.com (Chinaberry has great book reviews.)

www.cobblestonepub.com (Click on "For Kids" to publish student writing.)

www.connect2earth.org (World Wildlife Fund's site for student articles/text, images, and videos; each submission rated by viewers.)

http://depts.washington.edu/pswrite/responding.html (Tips for responding to student writing.)

www.discover-writing.com/forstudents.html (Submissions for student writing contests and publications, as well as some terrific topic ideas.)

http://dsc.discovery.com (The Discovery Channel site overflows with clever mini-segments related to science and social studies.)

www.educationworld.com/a_tech/tech/tech042.shtml (Many links for publishing students' writing online, plus good teaching ideas and lesson plans.)

www.edutopia.org (Site is full of forward-thinking articles and meaningful writing prompts, no doubt the pride of its founders, the George Lucas Foundation.)

www.enn.com/news/enn-stories (The Environmental News Network with daily updates on a variety of issues for middle schoolers.)

www.envirocitizen.org (National Environmental Wire for Students.)

www.greenhour.org (A website to link home, school, and science; lots of info from journal entries to make-and-dos to topic-related books.)

www.greenpeace.org (An environmental site with interesting articles and sample petitions.)

http://home.earthlink.net/~jhholly/gradualrelease.htm (A helpful site for understanding the gradual release model of instruction.)

www.kidshealth.org (The latest on everything from chicken pox to dyslexia in easy-to-read articles for kids and by kids.)

www.literacymatters.org/tech/write.htm (A ton of information related to "cybercomp," interactive web pages, web writing, electronic portfolios, lesson plans, and lots more.)

www.merlynspen.org (Stories and articles by kids for kids.)

http://ncset.uoregon.edu (Information, guidelines, and other support from the National Center for Supported e-Text.)

www.NPR.org (National Public Radio is overflowing with short pieces of writing and audios.)

www.nrich.maths.org.uk (Great source for math problems, games, and articles, including some to challenge those gifted minds.)

www.panda.org (The World Wildlife Fund's comprehensive website for youth, with articles about people, places, science, and other subjects.)

www.PBS.org (Public Broadcasting System has a bounty of short, current pieces of writing and audios.)

www.pitara.com/magazine/features.asp (A wonderful website and magazine from India with many great articles/essays published by kids.)

www.readwritethink.org (Sponsored by IRA, NCTE, and Verizon, this site offers tons of reading and language arts resources, such as lesson plans, articles, and much more.)

www.sierraclub.org (Sierra Club is tops for environmental information.)

http://www.stackthedeck.com/samples.html (Samples of students' writing that can be used for assessment examples.)

www.stonesoup.com (Listen to or read stories written by kids for kids.)

http://www.teachervision.fen.com/lesson-plan/reading-comprehension/48701.html (Over 100 graphic organizers. From prefix webs to analogy organizers to centimeter grids, it's all here!)

http://www.thepetitionsite.com (A great site for model petitions sponsored by Care2 and related to topics that interest and excite kids.)

http://thewritesource.com/models.htm (A great source for models of student writing from a variety of genres, from creative to factual.)

www.timeforkids.com (*Time* magazine for grades 4–7.)

www.teenink.com (Terrific articles, essays, and reviews written by kids for everyone.)

www.thinkquest.org (ThinkQuest is a terrific global network of students, teachers, parents, and technologists dedicated to exploring youth-centered learning. Its online library includes over 6,500 websites created by students around the world who have participated in a ThinkQuest Competition.)

www.tnc.org (Sponsored by The Nature Conservancy with lots of good articles.)

http://www.ttms.org (A ton of writing-related information for teachers.)

www.ttms.org/PDFs/03%20Writing%20Samples%20v001%20(Full).pdf (Downloadable pages of student writing, which would be good to use for common assessment.)

www.webenglishteacher.com/publish.html (Ideas for publishing and places to publish student writing as well as lesson plans, author biographies, and more.)

www.wikipedia.com (An evolving online encyclopedia that is continually updated by experts around the world.)

Websites for Sample Constructed-Response (CR) Items and Student Writing Samples from State Assessments

State Web Sites

AL – Alabama (No CR samples or examples found.)

AK – Alaska
www.eed.state.ak.us/tls/assessment/SBA_ItemSamplers.html (Examples from all subjects, well organized.)

AZ – Arizona
www.ade.az.gov/standards/AIMS/SampleTests/ (Writing only.)

AR – Arkansas
www.arkansas.gov (PDF files.)

CA – California
(Uses only multiple-choice tests in all subjects, including writing.)

CO – Colorado
www.cde.state.co.us/cdeassess/released_items.html (CR examples from all
    subjects.)

CT – Connecticut (No CR samples or examples found.)

DE – Delaware
www.doe.k12.de.us/programs/aab/sample_items/default.shtml (CR samples
    and examples from all subjects with benchmarked responses.)

FL – Florida
http://fcat.fldoe.org/fcatit07.asp (Writing only.)

GA – Georgia
www.doe.k12.ga.us/ci_testing.aspx?PageReq=CITestingWA5 (Writing only.)

HI – Hawaii (No CR samples or examples found.)

ID – Idaho (No CR samples or examples found.)

IL – Illinois
www.isbe.state.il.us/assessment/htmls/sample_books.htm

IN – Indiana
www.doe.state.in.us/istep/publications.html

IA – Iowa (No CR samples or examples found.)

KS – Kansas (No CR samples or examples found.)

KY – Kentucky
http://education.ky.gov/KDE/HomePageRepository/Site+Map.htm

LA – Louisiana
http://www.doe.state.la.us/lde/saa/760.html

ME – Maine
http://www.maine.gov/education/mea/mearelitems.htm

MD – Maryland
http://mdk12.org/assessments/k_8/index_c.html

MA – Massachusetts
http://www.doe.mass.edu/mcas/testitems.html (One of the most accessible, comprehensive sites for constructed-response items and responses.)

MI – Michigan
http://www.michigan.gov/mde/0,1607,7-140-22709_31168---,00.html (A site with tons of samples of constructed-response items and benchmarked responses from across the curriculum.)

MN – Minnesota
http://education.state.mn.us/WebsiteContent/ResourcesFor.jsp?siteId=7&siteSection=Accountability+Programs%2FAssessment+and+Testing&audience=Teachers

MS – Mississippi (No CR samples or examples found.)

MO – Missouri
http://dese.mo.gov/divimprove/assess/Released_Items/riarchiveindex.html (Reading examples categorized to nonfiction, fiction, and poetry; site moving into more constructed response.)

MT – Montana
http://www.opi.state.mt.us/Assessment/Phase2.html#RI08 (Constructed response in each subject, along with benchmarked responses.)

NE – Nebraska (Moving from school-based to state-based assessment, so no online resources are available yet.)

NV – Nevada
http://www.doe.nv.gov/statetesting/critreftests.html
(Organized, easy-to-use site.)

NH – New Hampshire
http://www.ed.state.nh.us/education/doe/organization/curriculum/NECAP/Released%20Items/2006ReleasedItems.htm (A comprehensive offering related to the New England Common Assessment Program.)

NJ – New Jersey

http://www.state.nj.us/education/assessment/es/ (Comprehensive with constructed response across the curriculum.)

NM – New Mexico (No CR samples or examples found.)

NY – New York

http://www.emsc.nysed.gov/osa/ (One of the most comprehensive and accessible sites for constructed-response prompts and responses in all curricular areas from a state that's used these for over a decade.)

NC – North Carolina (No CR samples or examples found.)

ND – North Dakota

http://www.dpi.state.nd.us/standard/asments/reading.shtm (Brief response prompts and benchmarked samples for reading.)

OH – Ohio

http://www.ode.state.oh.us/GD/Templates/Pages/ODE/ODEDetail.aspx?page=3&TopicRelationID=1070&ContentID=7479&Content=46112 (A state with long-standing experience using written response items, which can be found in every subject, along with tons of online samples.)

OK – Oklahoma (Samples for writing only, but minimal.)

OR – Oregon (No CR samples or examples found.)

PA – Pennsylvania

http://www.pde.state.pa.us/a_and_t/cwp/view.asp?a=108&Q=73314&a_and_tNav=|680|&a_and_tNav=| (Lots of examples, even some with extended response items.)

RI – Rhode Island

http://www.ride.ri.gov/Assessment/necap_science.aspx (Examples from each subject using the New England Common Assessment Program.)

SC – South Carolina

http://ed.sc.gov/agency/offices/assessment/pact/PACTReleaseItems.html (Uses constructed response, but examples are minimal; site being updated.)

SD – South Dakota (No CR samples or examples found.)

TN – Tennessee (No CR samples or examples found.)

TX – Texas
http://www.tea.state.tx.us/student.assessment/resources/release/taks/index.
html (Quite a few examples for reading, including some in Spanish.)

UT – Utah (No CR samples or examples found.)

VT – Vermont
http://education.vermont.gov/new/html/pgm_assessment/necap/resources/
released_items.html#07 (Reading and writing samples from New England
Common Assessment Program.)

VA – Virginia (All assessments are multiple choice, including writing.)

WA – Washington
http://www.k12.wa.us/ (Use pull-down menu for Assessment to find constructed-response prompts, answers, and benchmarked examples for all
subjects; definitely a sophisticated site.)

WV – West Virginia (No CR samples or examples found.)

WI – Wisconsin
http://dpi.wi.gov/oea/wkce.html (A few examples from all subjects.)

WY – Wyoming (No samples or examples found.)

BIBLIOGRAPHY

Allen, J. 2008. "Read Our Walls: Bridging Professional Development and Student Achievement." Choice Literacy. http://www.choiceliteracy.com/public/606.cfm.

Begley, S. 2007. *Train Your Mind and Change Your Brain*. New York: Ballantine/Random House.

Blume, J. 1972. *Tales of a Fourth-Grade Nothing*. New York: Dell.

Cambourne, B. 1988. *The Whole Story: Natural Learning and the Acquisition of Literacy in the Classroom*. New York: Scholastic.

Canfield, J., and M. V. Hansen. 1993. *Chicken Soup for the Soul: 101 Stories to Open the Heart and Rekindle the Spirit*. Deerfield Beach, FL: Health Communications.

Canfield, J., M. V. Hansen, M. Donnelly, C. Donnelly, and J. Tunney. 2000. *Chicken Soup for the Sports Fan's Soul: 101 Stories of Insight, Inspiration and Laughter from the World of Sports*. Deerfield Beach, FL: Health Communications.

Carroll, L. 2000. *Alice's Adventures in Wonderland.* New York: Signet.

Chomsky, N. 2008. *The Essential Chomsky.* New York: New Press.

Cole, A. 2003. *Knee to Knee, Eye to Eye: Circling in on Comprehension.* Portsmouth, NH: Heinemann.

Dahl, R. 2005. *Charlie and the Chocolate Factory.* New York: Puffin.

Dillard, A. 1989. *The Writing Life.* New York: Harper & Row.

Eisner, E. W. 1991. *The Enlightened Eye: Qualitative Inquiry and the Enhancement of Educational Practice.* New York: Macmillan.

Elbow. P. 1981. *Writing with Power: Techniques for Mastering the Writing Process.* New York: Oxford.

Flanigan, R. L. 2005. "Fourth-Graders' Literacy Improving: School 20 Gets an 'A' for Literacy Effort." *Democrat and Chronicle* (Rochester, NY), May 19.

Fletcher, R. 2000. *How Writers Work: Finding a Process That Works for You.* New York: HarperCollins.

Fox, M. 1993. *Radical Reflections: Passionate Opinions on Teaching, Learning, and Living.* New York: Harcourt Brace.

Gardner, H. 1993. *Frames of Mind: The Theory of Multiple Intelligences.* New York: Basic Books.

Graves, D. H. 1983. *Writing: Teachers and Children at Work.* Portsmouth, NH: Heinemann.

Harvey, S. 1998. *Nonfiction Matters: Reading, Writing, and Research in Grades 3–8.* Portland, ME: Stenhouse.

Harvey, S., and A. Goudvis. 2007. *Strategies That Work: Teaching Comprehension for Understanding and Engagement.* 2nd ed. Portland, ME: Stenhouse.

Hindley, J. 1996. *In the Company of Children.* Portland, ME: Stenhouse.

Holly, J. "Compendium of Instructional Strategies." http://home.earthlink.net/~jhholly/gradualrelease.htm.

Kane, T. 1988. *The Oxford Guide to Writing*. New York: Oxford University Press.

King, S. 2000. *On Writing: A Memoir of the Craft*. New York: Scribner.

Kohn, A. 2000. *A Case Against Standardized Testing: Raising the Scores, Ruining the Schools*. Portsmouth, NH: Heinemann.

LaGasse, P., ed. 1994. *Concise Columbia Encyclopedia*. 3rd ed. New York: Columbia University Press.

Lamott, A. 1994. *Bird by Bird: Some Instructions on Writing and Life*. New York: Anchor Books.

Montgomery County BOCES. 2005. "Taking the Mystery Out of the Writing Process." *Wells Central School News*, spring.

National Center for Education Statistics. 2007. "Sample Questions Booklets: Mathematics and Reading at Grade 4—Part 2." http://nces.ed.gov/nationsreportcard/about/booklets.asp.

National Public Radio. "Novelist Stephen King" (audio file). *NPR.org*. http://www.npr.org/templates/story/story.php?storyid=1112273.

Neufeldt, V., ed. 1991. *Webster's New World Dictionary*, 3d ed. New York: Simon & Schuster.

Nye, N. S. 1994. "Valentine for Ernest Mann." In *Red Suitcase*. Brockport, NY: BOA Editions.

Pearson, P. D., and Gallagher, M. C. 1983. "The Instruction of Reading Comprehension." *Contemporary Educational Psychology* 8:317–344.

The Phantom Professor. "Writing Workshop Lesson 7: In the Zone." The Phantom Professor. http://phantomprof.blogspot.com/2005/09/writing-workshop-lesson-7-in-zone.html

Routman, R. 1996. *Literacy at the Crossroads: Crucial Talk About Reading, Writing, and Other Teaching Dilemmas*. Portsmouth, NH: Heinemann.

Saunders, S. 2001. "Backlash Building Against State Tests." *New York Teacher*, June 6.

Scieszka, J. 1996. *The True Story of the Three Little Pigs!* New York: Puffin.

Smith, F. 1982. *Writing and the Writer*. New York: Holt, Rinehart, and Winston.

———. 1987. *Joining the Literacy Club: Further Essays into Education*. Portsmouth, NH: Heinemann.

Wilder, L. E. [1935] 2004. *Little House on the Prairie*. New York: HarperTrophy.

Woolridge, S. 1997. *Poemcrazy*. New York: Three Rivers Press.

Vygotsky, L. 1978. *Mind and Society*. Cambridge, MA: Harvard University Press.